CORPORATE WISDOM IN TIRUKKURAL

M Rajaram

Vitasta

Published by
Renu Kaul Verma
Vitasta Publishing Pvt Ltd
2/15, Ansari Road, Daryaganj
New Delhi - 110 002
info@vitastapublishing.com

ISBN 978-93-86473-11-0

Fist Edition 2017
2nd Reprint 2019
MRP ₹399

Cover and layout by Vits Press
Printed by Vikas Computer and Printers

Dedicated

to

Good Governance

Acknowledgements

In recognition of the hard work that has gone into writing this book, I would like to thank my most dear friends S Velliyangiri, P K Natarajan, J Narayanaswamy, C S Kalyanasundaram, R G Rajaram, P Jeyaraj, David Balasingh, V Rajagopal and others for all their active support.

Contents

Publisher's Note

Thirukkural was written 2000 years ago. Thiruvalluvar who gave us *Thirukkural*, the book for all ages, was an eminent and exceptional scholar.

Thirukkural is recognised as a classic in world literature. It is not only a work of great aesthetic and literary value but also a guide to the art of living, with nuggets of valuable wisdom on management sprinkled everywhere. All the 'kurals' deal with various aspects of human activities like devotion to God, ascetic life, family life, charity, kingship, defence, friendship, love etc.

Thirukkural covers subjects like ethics, statecraft, citizenship etc in myriad forms. It is a book on management applicable to corporates too. The sage's thoughts on management are appealing to the mind, sweet to the ear and delicious to the tongue. We can say, 'Age cannot wither it nor custom stale its infinite variety'.

The dynamics of *Thirukkural* have been richly complimented by various scholars. Mahatma Gandhi called it 'a textbook of indispensable authority on moral life' and goes on to say, 'The maxims of Valluvar have touched my soul. There is no one who has given such a treasurehouse of wisdom like him'. He also said that he came to know about *Thirukkural* from Leo Tolstoy, who had said that the concept of non-violence and humanism was taken by him from a German version of the kurals. And so he expressed his desire to learn Tamil, so as to be able to study *Thirukkural* in the original.

It deals with good governance and management in general, organisational relations, leadership qualities, domestic relations, social relations, public relations, communication skills, human resource management, project management, financial management, decision making and some case studies applicable in everyday situations.

This book, *Corporate Wisdom,* will surely be a guide for all people in various walks of life, especially leaders in the corporate world and in government.
In many ways, it paves the path to success and happiness. It provides a lot of tips on management.

from APJ Abdul Kalam
as President of India

In the words of President Kalam

We must build a strong, positive self image. It's easy to say to ourselves that something can't be done but really we are recalling times when we tried and the result was not good and limiting our own growth because of the failure. We must seek to build an unrestricted view of achievements. Now!

A great entrepreneurial thinker, M Rajaram, IAS quotes 11 basic points that waste time and drain a positive approach. It is essential we avoid: Being anxious about the future; reliving the past; regretting earlier mistakes; brooding yesterday's events; concerned over impermanence; resisting change.

Anticipating tomorrow and racing against time, we need to remove the fear of failure and realise that there are no failures, only events and outcomes. Then we evaluate why things happened that way and try again with a positive heart. It's a fact that whatever we do we always get a result. It's just not always the one we want. We have to keep on trying like Thomas Alva Edison to succeed, making failures as steps to success.

Foreword

Thiruvalluvar was one of the greatest poets and visionaries that our country has ever produced. His collection of 1,330 kurals or couplets is as relevant today as it was 2000 years ago, when it was originally penned. His work encapsulates age-old wisdom about trade, commerce, employment, governance, virtues etc. which drove India to become one of the greatest civilisations of the world centuries ago.

As any other Tamil boy, I was exposed to *Thirukkural* since early childhood and I was excited when I received and read the book, *Corporate Wisdom*, for it encapsulates all the principles that I have followed in my life.

Dr M Rajaram is a leading Tamil and English scholar and also an alumni of my alma mater, the PSG College of Technology in Coimbatore. He has successfully compiled the evergreen verses of Thiruvalluvar in this book. It is relevant for all those who want to make a mark in the field of management or want to pursue a successful career across any field.

This book deals with philosophies of governance and management in general and the virtue of pursuing commerce and trade while still following the path of righteousness. It emulates the whole spectrum of underlying principles that guide organistional function and growth from public relations, leadership qualities to governance. My own entrepreneurial journey has taught me that good governance is the key to laying the foundation of a successful business.

The examples and case studies that Rajaram has used are simple and easily relatable and will serve as excellent guide when the readers are faced with difficult situations in the course of running their enterprises.

Shiv Nadar

Founder and Chairman,

HCL and Shiv Nadar Foundation

Author's Note

During the latter half of 19th century when industrialisation was in full swing in the western countries, coupled with exploitation of the employees which was rampant in the rush for making profits, leading thinkers like Max Weber were greatly concerned with improving industrial output on the one hand, and, arresting the exploitation of the working force on the other.

Weber, the German scholar and renowned sociologist, formalised the concept of bureaucracy. His proposition was to arrest the crudities of the entrepreneurs towards the employees and to systematise the various facets of management and enterprise. He designed a rational structure of organisation in which work could be carried out in an orderly manner and the employees could give their best to their work. At the same time, they would be fully protected by this system.

In this system, the work at each level is clearly defined and the rights and obligations of the employee are laid down in clear-cut terms. And the organisation can be managed with greater efficiency.

Bureaucratic organisations in governments and corporate houses are considered as rational and legal systems. The manager or the administrator derives his authority and power from a legitimised source which is known to all people in the organisation. Appointment in any post is done by merit, based on objective criteria laid down for the purpose. The position is more important than the person holding it.

Continuity in administration is ensured in this system with standing rules and regulations and by the written records of many years of past precedence. Constant training of people ensures efficiency in the organisation.

The bureaucratic organisation confers the right to appeal to the competent authority on any decision that the employee considers unjustifiable or biased and as such, he need not fear any reprisal from his superior.

In spite of so many advantages, there are weaknesses in this bureaucratic system of organisation such as red-tapism, premium on mediocrity and moulding the individuals with high potential to just a stereotype. But still, bureaucracy has seldom been successfully substituted in business or government.

Developing countries like India have taken the lead from western literature of business management and public administration. But, after independence from colonial rule, most developing countries have had to indulge in a great deal of discussion about changes in organisational structure and management practices because of the rapid growth in demand for products and services.

Moreover, administrators have understood that culture and tradition of a society have much influence on management practices.

Organisations in Japan are very different from those in the United Kingdom. In Japan much importance is given for the peer level and hierarchical level consultations for functional specialisation, team work with spontaneous cooperation.

The base on which an effective administrative system has to be designed is a deep understanding of the human behaviour and motive. The employee's reaction to work and to its varied factors is largely derived from the background and culture prevailing in the society.

The concepts of good behaviour and misbehaviour, punctuality and keeping to schedules, subordination and super ordination, exercising power and authority etc. have to be conceived in accordance with cultural orientation.

As far as India is concerned, it is a country of villages and more than seventy per cent of India's population live in rural areas. The extended family system, traditional systems, traditional customs and habits etc prevailing in India demand some modified practices from the western management system, especially in respect of supervision, discipline, delegation, control systems etc.

In order to venture on a project that will showcase the importance of evolving a modified administrative system to suit the age-old tradition and culture, I have taken *Thirukkural,* a classic created by Thiruvalluvar 2000 years ago, as a frame of reference.

Thirukkural is a moral treatise meant for all of mankind. The lofty aim of Thiruvalluvar is to show to mankind the way to a wholesome life.

Though Thiruvalluvar has been understood as a sage, a seer, a philosopher or as a spiritual leader, he is not confined to any one plane. He is interested in the wholeness of human life. He speaks about virtuous life, domestic life and material life. He speaks about the full-fledged country; about the king and his army. He also speaks about romantic love and celibacy. In life, even romance and sex have an ethical dimension. Thiruvalluvar does not have segmental views on human life. He sees life in its totality and wholeness.

He speaks about the duties and responsibilities of king and his palace officials. He speaks about the various welfare activities required for a welfare state, about effective delegation, and about some of the most important basic human factors of public administration.

The ancient poet-seer is said to have lived in Tamil Nadu about 2000 years ago. No authentic details about his actual span of life, place of birth, his family and his life-style are available. He is known by his classical ethic, *Thirukkural.*

'Kural' means anything short and crisp. In Tamil prosody it is used to refer to a short poetic form of one and three-fourth of a line of a couplet containing a single complete idea. This epigrammatic form is a difficult medium which is rarely attempted by any other poet for such a work as *Thirukkural.*

Thirukkural contains 1,330 couplets in 133 chapters, each containing 10 couplets. Each chapter is headed by one major factor of human life such as Family Life, Goodness of Life Mate, Bliss of Children etc. Ten couplets under each chapter expounds the various aspects of the particular factor in depth, clarity and its wholeness. This work is divided into three major heads – (1) On Righteous Life (2) On Material Life (3) On Love Life.

Thiruvalluvar communicates his luminous insights and wisdom by embracing humanity as a whole. Each and every word of his kural (couplets) is supercharged with deep meaning. In one kural, he says, the more one learns the greater he becomes aware of his ignorance. This phrase is very much applicable in the case of one's learning of *Thirukkural* itself. Students of *Thirukkural* have to squeeze every word and phrase and strive to capture its meaning little by little, gradually. G U Pope who translated *Thirukkural* into English metric verses in 1886 explains poetically about the difficulty in deriving the meaning of the kurals in the following words: *Their construction resembles that of a design in mosaic, the materials fitted together are sometimes mere bits of coloured glasses, but, sometimes also very precious stones and pure gold. You walk round it, and try to catch it in all lights, and feel at first, and often for long time as if it meant nothing at all, till you catch some hint, and at once it lies revealed, something to be thought of again; and again some bit of symbolism it may be, not infrequently grotesque, often quaint but sometimes also of rare beauty.*

Many scholars of *Thirukkural* have written commentaries on it and made translations into other languages. The very fact that there are still fresh commentaries and new interpretations forthcoming from numerous scholars and also that there are many scholars contradicting each other in their interpretation of a number of 'kurals' and in expounding 'Valluvam' (the concept of Thiruvalluvar) is illustrative of the fact that *Thirukkural* has to be understood and projected to the world after intensive research and study.

One of the reasons for the contradiction between these scholars of *Thirukkural* is that every such scholar sees the 'Valluvam' in accordance with his own religious or social outlook. They fail to cherish the fact that 'Valluvam' is a non-religious and universal scheme of a perfect human life. Thiruvalluvar has not imagined a Utopia or a heaven for human beings to simply aspire for. He has not dwelt upon any abstract thoughts or dogmas. He is out and out concerned with the practical world wherein the despicable as well as the noble, the begging lot as well as the wealthy lot, hypocrites as well as the honest are all dwelling side by side. Thiruvalluvar is projecting his firm belief and conviction that society can be so elevated and cultured as to serve as an abode for all human beings where they lead a healthy, wealthy and wise life. With this lofty vision in his mind, he prescribes duties and responsibilities to the people in all walks of life.

He is solely concerned with the present world. To him, how one is living at present is a matter of supreme importance. He advocates strenuous efforts as the criterion of one's life, irrespective of the result whether one succeeds or fails. Thiruvalluvar does not consider the ascetic life anything better than conjugal life. As a matter of fact, a life of austerity and renunciation is placed only next to domestic life. He is particular that in this life there is full participation in this world with all its vagaries, glory or tragedy. The human kind will be elevated as a result of virtuous life.

In order to enable readers who have not known Thiruvalluvar and his classic *Thirukkural*, to understand more about them, the considered opinion and compliments of great men of eminence on the *Thirukkural* are quoted here:

Albert Schweitzer

With sure strokes, the 'kural' draws the ideal of simple ethical humanity. There hardly exists in the literature of the world a collection of maxims in which we find so much of lofty wisdom.

Aurobindo

Thirukkural is a gnomic poetry, the greatest in plan, conception and force of execution ever written in this kind, of the Tamil saint, Thiruvalluvar.

M Ariel (the French savant)

A masterpiece of Tamil literature, one of the highest and purest expressions of human thought.

Rajaji

Thiruvalluvar's approach to moral doctrine is marked by a very thorough knowledge of human psychology and desire to help imperfect men with practical hints in the struggle against evil. Throughout, we can see how the poet brings everything down to the level of practicality without losing the ideals.

Yogi Shuddhananda Bharati

Thirukkural is a grand mosaic of cultural creation, a repertory of universal thoughts and truths. It is the one book for all, for all times, and a world that lives it shall enjoy eternal peace, harmony, health, wealth, power, grace and bliss. It gives the light of right life, the wealth of practical wisdom, the milk of hearts, abundance, the honey of conjugal bliss and the joy of peace and harmony at home and at wider homeland. It's the gospel of 'love and give', a code of a soul-luminous life. The whole human aspiration is epitomised in this immortal book—a book for all the ages.

Mahatma Gandhi

I want to learn Tamil language so that I can read *Thirukkural* in original and appreciate the treasure of wisdom in it.

K M Munshi

Thirukkural is a poetic composition of great antiquity in Tamil literature. Many great minds have shed their powerful, radiant light on this gem and justly famous classic of Tamil literature. In its essence, *Thirukkural* is a treatise par excellence on the art of living. Thiruvalluvar, the author, diagnoses the intricacies of human natures with such penetrating insight, perfect mastery and consummate skill absorbing the most subtle concepts of modern psychology. His prescription on godliness, ethics, morality and humanness are sagacious and practical to the core. They cut across castes, creeds, climes and ages and have a freshness which makes one feel as if they are meant for the present times.

G U Pope

Sage Valluvar, priest of thy lovely clan, no tongue repeats, no speech reveals thy name; yet, all things changing, dieth not thy fame for thou art bard of universal man.

Justice S Mahajan

His writings leave us the impression that he had a strong conviction that compassion is the power that holds the different parts of the universe together and the greatest happiness can only come from, and the perfect morality could consist in, a sensitive loyalty to the whole.

T P Meenakshi Sundaram (Ex-Vice Chancellor of Madurai Kamaraj University)

Ahimsa scrupulously practiced by the Jains, the compassion governing the acts of the Buddhists and the Satyagraha, the life principle of Mahatma Gandhi—these three explain much more than any commentary, the underlying principle of 'kural'.

V Kalynasundaram (the essayist)

Thirukkural is just like a 'mine' from which the things that have so far been taken out is only a little, very little. For this modern world and for the future world there is a lot of wisdom embedded in it. This mine is perennial.

M Varadharajan (Ex-Vice Chancellor of Madurai Kamaraj University)

Thirukkural is the treatise useful for varied people in a varied manner. Literary scholars can take it as a literary classic and learn its literary features. The savants and men of virtue can take it as a spiritual treatise and learn the orderly virtues. The politicians may take it as a political manual and learn the techniques required for them.

V S Manickam (Ex-Vice Chancellor of Madurai Kamaraj University)

Thirukkural is one of the classics which speaks on the practicality of virtues, while embracing the many facets of human life. It asserts the fact that one's development or otherwise is within one's own self and attracts all at any level in life. It formalises ways and means for the people to lead a life in harmony with the world.

Zakir Hussain, the former President of India, says, '*Thirukkural* is a treasurehouse of worldly knowledge, ethical guidance and spiritual wisdom'.

The Art of Good Governance

Thiruvalluvar and Public Administration

READERS MAY wonder as to how the precepts of Thiruvalluvar who lived 2000 years ago have any relevance at all to the modern management systems in public administration.

The head political administrator in any country in those days was a King or an Emperor as against the President or Prime Minister in the modern democratic world. But the fundamental facets of public administration have not changed with the passage of time so much as to contradict the public management that was in vogue in those days of monarchy.

Hence, the 'King' of those days as the head of political administration of monarchy can be replaced by the present-day President or Prime Minister; King's officials who were looking after the countries' welfare activities be replaced with the modern-day Corporate President, Chief executive or administrator. Quantum of power and authority between present-day administrators and a personnel of defunct monarchies may not be the same. But the basic duties and responsibilities of bureaucrats, norms of behaviour in specific situations, subordination and superordination, organisation and administration, delegation, inter-personal relations and the like could not ever change with the passage of time, hence the basic precepts for officials as rendered by Thiruvalluvar can as well be considered a valuable study material for innovative students of management.

However, the fact that Thiruvalluvar was a Tamil and Dravidian by race cannot be ignored. T R Sesha Iyengar, in his book *Dravidians' India*, says that Dravidians had already developed a civilisation of their own, long before the Aryan civilisation was transplanted in their mind. The Dravidians had been in possession of India long before the Aryans entered it. They established mighty kingdoms in the North and South.

It can be asserted that Thiruvalluvar sees humanity as a whole without any alienation by cast, creed or religion. Also Thiruvalluvar's ethics is meant for all the world communities. Public administration must rest upon a philosophy of service to humanity which has to inspire a high morale among its practitioners. 'The public official must live to serve before he serves to live.'

Our good old *Veda*s and *Upanishad*s, besides the inimitable *Bhagavad Gita* and *Arthashastra*, teach us a lot of management techniques. If we can go through them purposefully, we can understand them to the hilt and apply these techniques in our day-to-day professional and personal lives. Our belief, efforts and attitudes bring success to our doorsteps.

Hence, the basics of public administration derived from *Thirukkural* and expounded in this treatise, is a pioneer venture and has a high utility value for devising a modified administrative system for developing countries like India.

This book is not meant to create any illusion that, with the help of *Thirukkural* alone, anybody can govern a state or organise a secretariat or an army in the modern world. For that, we require various rules and regulations, standing orders, civil codes and numerous manuals and the like. Some of these rules and regulations are found in Kautilya's *Arthashastra*. But their practicability is no longer valid. 'They have become antiquated.' Timeless wisdom of Thiruvalluvar in not having dealt with any subject in any great details can therefore be understood. He concentrates himself on the unchanging realities of human nature and the eternal varieties of life.

Thiruvalluvar might not have contemplated the modern democracy but his basic human approach makes his work best fitted for any democratic government.

In the modern conception of the democratic world, the state exists for peoples' welfare, which Thiruvalluvar interprets in the widest sense of the term that is 'Virtue', the power of goodness which includes human perfection. Hence, the government and its administration have to be subsidiary to Virtue in as much as it has to create proper environment, social and material, for the achievement of perfection by the citizenry. All the other limbs of the state have to be charities while it's citizens are the beneficiaries. They exist, for the sake of the citizens and for enabling them to live a wholesome and perfect life. Hence, while speaking about a welfare state, Thiruvalluvar categorically asserts:

If land lacks love between King and subjects,
all its blessings are worthless.

Kural 740

Moving with the Boss

IN THE official hierarchy of public administration, the line of functions and responsibilities with the inherent power is a straight line. This line is known as the line of control or the line of command. Orders are passed down from the top level administrator to the lower level Managers and subordinates step by step.

The superior-subordinate relationship is absolute and unchallengeable. The direction of this command proceeds along the line of control towards the official goal, which is to be achieved by all the staff as a team.

Any dilution or diffusion of responsibilities or power in the line of control would cause confusion, and result in maladministration.

Each officer has to exercise care and tact while moving with his immediate superior and also while dealing with his subordinates. This element of human behaviour is the first and foremost factor for any government officer in public administration to function effectively.

Some of the subordinate officers who may be experts in their specified field may, at times, think that it is not proper for their 'boss' to attempt to control any of their own jobs when he has not had any experience in that particular job. These subordinates will be under the impression that the top-level administrator should have known each and everything before reviewing their work. This sort of feeling is absurd. The superior officers will be having broader exposure to society and wider responsibilities. They will be more generalists than being specialists in any particular field.

The subordinate officer has to understand very clearly that he should subordinate to his superior in all respects. He must accept full responsibility conferred on him and assist his superior in all his work. Besides the legitimate adherence to the line or authority, a subordinate officer has to exercise care and tact in maintaining good relations with his superior in all possible ways.

There are many such psychological factors to be considered in this respect. The precepts of Thiruvalluvar, though rendered 2000 years ago for the king and officials of the kingdom, are found to be very relevant and valuable for the present-day administrators as well, since the mode of functions of the human mind has not changed much with the passage of time.

Keep Optimum Distance

The officials serving the king (the superior) of varying temperament should neither get very close to him nor remain far away. Let them keep themselves at an optimum distance, just like those who warm themselves near the flame of fire.

Kural 691

People who warm themselves by making a camp fire during cold weather know the distance at which they have to keep themselves so as to derive adequate warmth. If they go too near the flame, they can get burnt, if they remain far away, they will not derive the required warmth.

The superior officer is analogous to the flame of fire. Because of substantial power vested in him by virtue of his higher position in the line of authority, he may be like a flame of fire to his subordinates. Otherwise, he may not be able to exercise sufficient control over them and he himself will become a misfit in the line of authority. Amidst his varied responsibilities and his broader exposure to government and society, he will be more and more sensitive and hence he may often be temperamental.

As such, a subordinate officer would do well if he considers his superior a flame of fire. If he chooses to go very near him, the superior is likely to feel displeased or hurt. He may think that he is under-valued by the subordinate or not properly respected.

But, on the other hand, if the subordinate keeps himself away from the superior, then again some other adverse feelings may arise in the mind of the superior. He may think that the subordinate is too egoistic to see him. Sometimes, it may also happen that if a subordinate officer keeps himself away from his superior, his colleagues or even his own subordinates will resort to slandering him before the superior.

Besides these adverse effects, the subordinate officer will not be able to function effectively and fulfill his responsibilities if he is not in sufficient touch with his superior.

Hence, the precept for a subordinate officer:
Consider your superior officer like the flame of fire. The flame will sway either way according to the wind-way. You can warm yourself by the flame of fire. Don't go too near or remain far away. Keep an optimum distance from your boss.

Respect Sensitivities of the Boss

Subordinates not to aspire for the things dear to the Boss.
It would merit superior's goodwill in their favour.
Kural 692

The superior officer has to be given pre-eminent place under whom all the subordinate officers and their staff become just the limbs of his superior position.

Not only should the methods of functioning of the superior but also his honest wishes and desires as well should be respected as unique features.

One or two examples will illustrate this aspect clearly.

The office vehicle can be legitimately utilised by the subordinate officer for official duties. But if the superior desires to have it by himself for his demi-official use, it is not advisable on the part of the subordinates to demand the vehicle. He should make alternate arrangements for his official travels. If he does so, even though he may face some hardship which is not legitimately warranted, he can capitalise on such hardship for securing the goodwill of the superior.

The superior officer, while on camp, may wish to go to a cinema theatre by himself to enjoy the film show. The subordinate officer accompanying him should understand his desire and keep himself away from the theatre. If he acts on the contrary, the superior cannot, of course, take disciplinary action against him for such matters. But the displeasure of the superior will be reflected in his official dealings concerning the subordinate.

This advice may sound silly but it is based on human psychology.

A superior officer endowed with enormous power may become autocratic in many respects. The subordinates have to orient their behaviour only in accordance with the superior's will and pleasure.

So, the precept for a subordinate is:

Your cautious refraining from casting your desires on what your superior aspires will fetch you prosperity in the official hierarchy.

Avoid Whispering, Smiling

Refrain from whispering and smiling with your neighbour in the presence of the Great with superior power.

Kural 694

Let us assume that a subordinate officer is attending along with his peers a review meeting conducted by his superior. During the course of the meeting the subordinate officer may tend to communicate something personal to his neighbour. On such occasions, he may resort to whispering. During such private communication his companion or he himself may smile in glee or derision. These are all private matters, of course.

But what would be the reaction of the superior if he happens to notice such behaviour of his subordinate? When a subordinate is called upon for a review meeting or for some other discussion, he is expected to be wholly and exclusively attentive to the superior. The very act of the subordinate in communicating with his neighbour during the meeting will tend to mean that he is not at all attentive to the matter under discussion. And, that too, if added with whispering and smiling, will cause irritation and suspicion in the mind of the superior to the effect that either the subordinate is ignoring the subject matter of discussion or that he is criticising the very discussion.

Once suspected by the superior, it will be very difficult for the subordinate, however clever he may be, to set himself in right relationship with the superior.

So precept for a subordinate officer:

In order to safeguard himself, therefore, the subordinate must avoid any whispering or smiling in the presence of his superior or people of eminence.

Fish not any Secrets

Do not try to overhear any secret conversation, nor to fish out any secret matter. Await until it is let out in due course.

Kural 695

If a subordinate displays an inquisitiveness to know any secret of his superior, it may mean that he is trying to go beyond his limit and to encroach upon the private territory of his superior. If the superior happens to notice such behaviour of his subordinate, he will invariably suspect him. Then the dependability of the subordinate will be eroded and the result will be immensely harmful to him.

No subordinate can question his superior as to which matter has to be kept by him as a secret and which can be let out for the subordinate to know.

Moreover, every human being will have his own requirement of privacy and everybody may be having his own weaknesses in his private life. Intruding upon the privacy of even his wife by the husband or vice-versa is inconsistent with a civilised culture. That will cause resentment and hatred and spoil the otherwise good relationship.

Every movement of the superior has to be duly respected by the subordinates. Any attempt to overhear his confidential conversation will be very unseemly a thing on the part of the subordinates who have to take every care to maintain a good relationship with their superior.

Hence, the precept for the subordinate is:

The supremacy will be reflected in each and every act of the superior. Hence his secret conversation, or for that matter his private social behaviour should also be valued with due respect. Trespassing upon his private territory will never be tolerated by the superior.

Don't Undervalue your Superior

Do not look down upon your superior on the plea that he is junior in service or he is your kinsman. Let your behaviour with him be strictly in accordance with his super authority and superiority.

Kural 698

A subordinate officer has to understand his own position with reference to his superior officer in the line of authority. When a higher authority promulgates an order, it becomes the duty of the subordinate to support that higher authority, to interpret such a decision to his own subordinates and to ensure their willing implementation of the same.

The decision of the superior should not be questioned on the plea that the superior is junior in service or that he is not having the requisite experience so as to decide on the particular issue or that he is an old colleague of the subordinate. Sometimes it may also happen that the superior is a kinsman of the subordinate.

It is quite irrelevant as to who is the person who occupies the higher position. It is only the post and not the particular person that actually matters in the line of authority, Men may come and men may go but the post remains as such.

Dilution of his power and authority by his subordinates will never be tolerated by any superior officer, whatever expertise the subordinate can exercise in his functioning, or, whatever qualification he may be possessing.

Necessary wisdom can be derived from the innumerable historical incidents in which brothers or other close kinsmen of the king were killed or removed from his territory only because those men failed to fall in line with the king's men to support the king's sovereignty.

So the important lesson for all officials in the official hierarchy is or the percept for a subordinate officer is:

Don't underestimate your higher authority or devalue his

superiority. May be he is less qualified or less experienced than you; he may be even your kinsman or your old companion. Forget all such passing facts; Keep it in your mind intact—He is the superior authority for you to orient your responsibility.

No Unseemly Acts

> *The clever-visioned officer, under the impression that he is held by his superior as his close confidant, will not do any unseemly things that would defame the superior.*
>
> Kural 699

Superior officer may keep some of his subordinates as his confidants, mainly for the purpose of strengthening his own authority and command over his field of operation. It is foolish on the part of any such subordinate to think that he has become so close to his superior that his closeness is indispensable for his boss. The very fact that one is held as a confidant by the superior should necessarily infuse in his mind more sense of duty and responsibility. He will be expected to be more and more vigilant so as to keep his closeness with his superior intact by exercising added care and subordination and make himself worthy of that closeness. If, on the other hand, the close associates resort to doing unseemly things which may result in a bad name for the superior in the department or among the public, then how long can such subordinates continue to remain close to him?

Actually, the superior would want his close confidant to more effectively carry out his directions. The subordinate should not choose to go in the opposite direction to do anything unbecoming of his position by taking undue advantage of his closeness with his superior. If he does so, that will not only impair the good name of his superior but the office morale also will go down. The resultant blow will strike down such an erring officer with a momentum proportionate to his erstwhile closeness with his superior. Numerous examples can be quoted for such happenings from both the political and civil administration.

Hence, the precept for a subordinate officer is:

Are you a close associate or a confidant of your superior? Be more careful and tactful. You're expected to subordinate more. Look not in the opposite direction so as to do any unseemly actions.

How to Call on Him?

On ascertaining his good humour and a favourable time, you must tell your superior such things that he may desire to hear.

Kural 696

No officer can keep himself away from his superior if he is to be an effective administrator. He will have to discuss with his superior frequently and seek his directions on administrative and technical matters if he is an executive as well as an administrator. He will have to bring to the notice of his superior any obstacles that may have cropped up in the way of his administration or execution of schemes and seek his advice then and there.

Similarly, he has to represent to his superior the needs and interests of his own subordinate staff. And in case of lapses and serious charges on the part of any of his subordinates, he has to report to his superior promptly.

Though he is entitled to contact his superior whenever necessity arises, he should not fix the time for the meeting arbitrarily by himself without caring for the convenience of his superior.

Whatever may be the pressure or the necessity and urgency of meeting the superior, it should always be kept in mind by the subordinate officer that the superior will be having more pressure of work and more responsibility. If one officer is feeling the urgency of meeting him, the superior will be having more number of such officers under his control. The work habits and the programme schedules of the superior must be closely observed and duly respected.

The superior, in turn, if he is a good administrator, does not discourage, but positively welcomes reports of any troublesome matters, least they should reach unmanageable dimensions before he hears of them.

But the superior may have his own choice of things to hear from his subordinates. He may be having his own timings to listen to the varied subjects. After all, the superior is also a human being with a mind filled with pleasure and displeasures, likes and dislikes, bias and prejudice. Hence the subordinate officer should give sufficient consideration as to which things he must tell him on a particular occasion and when to seek his guidance. That is to say, the subordinate officer must be attentive and observe not only the work-habits of his superior in order to find out the proper time for meeting him, but he should understand his mental habit also so as to choose the subject matter for discussion and the appropriate manner in which he must talk to him.

Hence, if you are a subordinate officer, and if you want to meet your superior for discussion:

Choose a favourable time to call on him. Observe his mood, ascertain it's good. Choose not things he may dislike. Tell him such things he would desire to hear.

The Good Administrator

IN MODERN society, an administrator has to attend to many different functions in a varied situations. It is therefore very difficult to delineate the character of a good administrator and to list out exhaustively all the necessary qualities that would characterise him.

In an administrator, any one attribute may be so marked as to offset the lack of other desirable attributes. And also, the relative importance of various qualities will vary with the institutional situations. For example, an officer who gets along with modest abilities in a long established organisation like a Directorate as one among numerous officers under the Director may miserably fail if he is placed to shoulder the responsibility of administering a separate office by himself.

But there are some basic factors essentially required for a good administrator. Out of these essential attributes, an effective administrator can be expected to have some admixture of half of them at least.

Without the basic character, other attributes are insufficient. Loyalty to the institution and a sense of dedication and an altruistic and idealistic outlook are some of the essential factors that would make a good administrator.

A good administrator has to administer good conduct, confidence and all the essential qualities among his subordinate staff in his office so as to build up a high office morale. Morale is essentially required in any administration for achieving the goal and ultimately in serving society.

Boats of Passion

Procrastination, forgetfulness, idleness and drowsy slumber are the four passion boats heading for doom.

Kural 605

Freedom from sloth is an essential requirement for any citizen to prosper in his domestic life. If any citizen fails to strive for his growth, he is bound to ruin his family. If this be the case in the narrow sphere of the family, what will happen if an administrator is cast in sluggishness, forgetfulness, laziness and procrastination? These undesirable elements on the part of anybody may act as a carrier of pleasure but will carry him to destruction ultimately.

'Do it now' is the motto of a good administrator. Procrastination, if allowed by any administrator to overtake his day-to-day work, he will not be able to dispose of anything in his office. He will simply add to his burden of work, multiply the problem and simply sleep with them. Such an administrator is a liability for the government and to society. The other pleasure boats of forgetfulness, languor and laziness are the different forms of slothfulness. An alert administrator will make quick decisions whenever required, step into action forthwith and activate all his staff to work as a dynamic team. He will be a morale-booster for his office staff. He will stabilise his position and power, gain more and more for his institution. The resultant gain towards his own growth will be proportionately high. Such an administrator is an asset both to the government and to the society.

Resoluteness in Action

The world will esteem no other power
but the will power to do whatever.

Kural 670

In the case of professional civil servants, simple willingness to take responsibility is what is expected of them. It reflects self-confidence. But this willingness must include courage, a readiness to take risks and a dynamic attitude.

The doers who are likely to carry responsibilities effectively are those who do not run away from them or avoid them despite their awareness that the responsibilities are heavy. They are the ones who know administration to be full of troubles and yet find it challenging and rewarding.

A civil servant in public administration may not be directly answerable to the public, but his performance of his duties in the implementation of a development scheme directly affects the welfare of the people. His poor performance or half-hearted functioning as an executive will mar the good name of the government and the ruling political party. If the administrator is not strong enough to hold full responsibility of the scheme he is entrusted with, and effectively implement the same unmindful of obstacles that may arise in his way, the public will discard the administration. That is to say that the general public will not require such administrators whether they are civil servants or political leaders.

The world shows interest in having only the tireless worker. In the case of public administration, a good administrator is one who is determined, with a strong will for resolute actions, with a sense of urgency and with his eyes on the deadline to complete his tasks on any account.

Action breeds action. A doer will never get rid of the multiplicity of actions. Hence Thiruvalluvar advocates uninterrupted action through whatever ways and wherever they are possible. If any project is struck through the feasible ways, action may be resorted to through some other way leading to success.

It is only action which actually builds ones conduct. The world welcomes only men of dynamic conduct. It prefers effective executives rather than arm-chair intellectuals or ivory tower philosophers.

Thiruvalluvar also advises the public administrators to strive in all possible ways to carry on every task to its successful completion.

If anybody shuns his work,
the world will not hesitate to shun him.

Kural 612

Be a Good Listener

One who listens and comprehends sharply will not,
even by slip, speak foolishly.

Kural 417

A good administrator needs to be a good listener. He will have to listen to the views of his subordinates and then initiate proper actions based on what he has listened to. He will ask searching questions and tap the answers from his subordinates which will illuminate the problems on hand in terms of his own responsibility.

Even the ablest subordinate will tend to discuss a problem in terms of his own involvement in it. The administrator listens in part to get the subordinate's views and in another part, he listens in order to identify things not said which will determine his own responsibility. He has then to inquire and comprehend about all those matters in accordance with his exposure to the larger part of his organisation.

The subordinate's view, in contrast, will be confined to narrower and more specialised functions. He is likely to lose some of his bearings because of his preoccupations with his techniques and other particulars.

Only by listening willingly and patiently the administrator can visualise the subordinate's views in a proper perspective and then guide the subordinate with proper directions.

The administrator will not err in his directions if he cultivates the habit of listening to his subordinate's views patiently and thoroughly without any reservation. He will not say any words foolishly, even by slip of the tongue.

But if an administrator does not listen to his subordinates properly, he is likely to err in his directions. His orders will sometimes be inconsistent with the actual requirement. Sometimes he may also speak foolishly. His administration will not be on a sound basis. Also the relationship between him and his subordinate staff will get disturbed, ultimately he will lose his overall command in the organisation.

Men to Reprove

An important practical hint for a good administrator is that he should prefer to have around him the ablest men he can find. He builds his own strength by building up the competence of his organisation, not by demonstrating how he can tower above incompetence.

A good administrator will have such strong self-confidence that it will enable him readily to confess ignorance and personal fault. But an incompetent administrator gets himself into frequent trouble by pretending to possess knowledge which he does not actually have. He will try to justify his least justifiable action.

Some of the subordinates may be more experienced and enlightened. To have such persons in close proximity will be the rarest of rare opportunities for a good administrator. That will strengthen his position.

Kural 443

The experienced persons around a good administrator will act as his eyes in his zone of administration and such men should be held in good poise.

Kural 445

They should be valued and kept in high esteem. They should be given the freedom to reprove the administrator himself whenever he goes wrong.

If there are no such people around him, so as to reprove him wherever he errs, even if there is no harmful enemies, the careless administrator is likely to ruin himself.

To give up good associates or subordinates is ten times worse for an administrator than being encircled by hostile people.

Kural 450

Hence, the precept for an administrator:

Have around you the ablest persons you can find. They will reprove and correct you when you run on.

Your position will be strengthened by them. Nobody can dislodge you then.

Considerateness

For those who would be gracious and considerate to all without detriment to their duties, this world will become their rightful place.

Kural 571

A good administrator should know how to be effective with his subordinates. He has to be skilled in avoiding personal offence, in knowing how to appease and also when to offend and persuade. He should be impersonal and fair towards each and every individual. He has to be considerate and defensive of his colleagues and subordinates.

He has also to be gracious and considerate to all but not at the cost of his legitimate duties. Even in the case of those who are offensive or harmful:

To show benignity and considerateness by the administrator will prove to be gainful in the long run.

Kural 579

In the evaluation of work turned out by a subordinate, if it is to be criticised, the administrator would do well if he tells it to the subordinate privately and not in the presence of other people. By so doing, the particular subordinate can be pulled up to productivity without causing him embarrassment or insult. Criticism in private will generally be productive. The subordinate will take the criticism in a positive sense and decide to correct himself willingly.

A good administrator should act as team worker. He should deal with his subordinates in a manner showing them the same kind of respect he himself gives to his superior. All are important to each other like the links in a chain.

A good administrator is considerate to others but never soft or gullible. He is a hard taskmaster but a fair one. He upholds the responsibility of his subordinates exactly as he wishes his own to be upheld.

Such considerateness on the part of an administrator will help him secure the wholehearted support and willing subordination of all his subordinate staff. Then his zone of control will become a rightful place for him. If he happens to be the Prime Minister or the political administrative head in a country, his zone of control is the country as a whole. Then the whole country will fall in line with his wishes. He can exercise his control throughout the country without having to face the least protest.

Such is the outcome of your considerateness. Let yours spring out from a sense of graciousness and, of course from dutifulness. You will have your right over this earth.

Lofty Will

Let your thoughts be elevated around a lofty will
even if it slips. It is still worth to have it intact.

Kural 596

One of the basic attributes of a promising administrator is his steadily enlarging ability to deal with more problems and more diverse people. It will be demonstrated in growing power. Such administrators can have a lofty will either to improve their organisation or to implement the rarely possible schemes to the betterment of the nation.

An ability to capitalise largely on relatively small experience is the essence of growing power. Some people may become more and more preoccupied with their repetitive experiences while others are enlightened by a particular experience to gain insights in various directions other than those already traversed by them.

Those of the second category have a certain capacity for generalising what they see and execute without becoming dogmatic. They are the ones who will be generating high ideals and lofty aims.

A good administrator is devoted to and enthusiastic in the performance of his duties. His enthusiasm with unceasing vigour and energy is his real wealth. It will be as great in proportion to his devotion to work. His enthusiasm and vibrant energy will be automatically transmitted to all his staff. He and his staff will be poised to carry out any hard task which will not normally be possible.

The stalks of water-flower are proportionate to the depth of water. So is men's greatness proportionate to their mental elevation.

Kural 595

Productivity will find its own way to the man of unfailing energy and diligence.

Kural 594

So an effective administrator is advised by Thiruvalluvar to have a strong will and great aims such as becoming himself an administrative head in his organisation or drafting a lofty welfare scheme so as to enhance the country's productivity.

Sometimes his noble aims might face a failure. But still, such an administrator and his team of staff will continue to be in elevated mental state in accordance with their lofty will and that is the real wealth in public administration.

Psychologically, a man becomes what he has in his mind. He is built up as per his thoughts. His great thoughts will ever keep him great.

Let all your thoughts be oriented towards noble aim and lofty will. Such aim and will may, at times, fail. But, you'd become part and parcel of it.

Laugh at Troubles

Laugh away when irksome troubles arise.
There is no other way for sliding them away.

Kural 621

An administrator who is to administer an office with a number of subordinate staff is not expected to react alarmingly whenever some troubles arise in the way of his administration. An administrator is not a mere individual any one of his subordinates. He has to be a role-model for the others to follow. He is therefore expected to develop by himself an attitude of equanimity on all occasions. Whenever he comes across any sorrowful incident or an irksome trouble, it is better for him to 'cultivate' the habit of laughing it away and not falling a prey to it.

It is a psychological fact that if one is depressed whenever a trouble arises, he will become prone to depression on the arrival of even minor troubles that can ordinarily be ignored, because sorrow breeds sorrow. And continual sorrowfulness will weaken the mind. But if one resorts to laughing at troubles, the sorrow will vanish in the absence of a shelter for it. An effective and clear-visioned administrator will not react negatively whenever he finds any impediment in the way of his functioning. He will ponder over the reason for the trouble and will try to rectify it.

A flood of troubles can be overcome by courageous thoughts entertained by the wise.

Kural 622

He will never experience sorrow who does not seek pleasure and who also considers distress as natural.

Kural 628

Sorrow does not come from outside. It is the product of one's mental attitude. Reacting alarmingly and undergoing mental depression whenever some troublesome incident occurs will spoil not only an executive's own mental equilibrium but will cause a negative leverage among his subordinate staff.

The Effective Executive

THERE IS not much difference between an administrator and an executive in public administration in India. The only difference is that an executive will be having the responsibility of implementing the public welfare schemes entrusted to him in addition to his administrative work.

This does not mean that an administrator is not concerned with the implementation of the government schemes. Actually, his administration has to be oriented towards the successful implementation of the various development schemes. Hence there is no clear-cut differentiation between an administrator and an executive in the present-day setup. But it can be mentioned that an executive is accountable more for his executive work even though a sound administration will help him implement the schemes successfully.

The output of an executive is actually the output of his organisation. The executive's own work is mainly important for the quantum of output of the organisation.

An executive is never done. Like a housewife, an executive's work is continuous. There will always be more to be done and more that can be done.

An executive is more an *actionist* than an administrator. He will carry out actions, multiply actions, delegate, supervise, guide and see that actions are being done and the project on hand is under steady progress. The executive has to act as a catalyst and activate his team at every stage of the project. He has to exercise a high degree of human management and psychology of the human behaviour. A cordial relation with all the members of his organisation is essential for the executive.

Thiruvalluvar deals with these basic factors from which every executive can derive the required inspiration so as to become more and more effective as an executive.

He speaks about mental strength, strong will, resoluteness of mind, sense of greatness etc. required for an executive. He also indicates as to how an executive can increase his leverage in his day-to-day activities as an executive, how to manage his time etc.

The precepts of Thiruvalluvar are all of general nature applicable to all the executives, wherever they may be functioning. All are fundamental requirements for each and every executive.

Mental Strength

Firmness of action is the firmness of mind.
All else are only external.

Kural 661

Each action of a man is positively or negatively affected by his mind. His actions have direct bearing on his mental functions. If he starts an action with a strong desire to do it, he does it effectively. But if he proceeds with indifference, his performance cannot be effective. Sometimes, he may not be able to complete it.

The mind has such a direct bearing with all living beings. If one is mentally weak, he is bound to be weak in his life; if he is strong, he will meet any eventuality firmly.

The same thing holds good in the case of an executive. If the executive is firmly determined to accomplish a task, successful accomplishment follows suit. Otherwise, an executive can never be effective.

In the absence of the firmness of mind, whatever resources an executive might be possessing—higher educational qualification, higher inherent wealth, convenient transport facilities and so on—he cannot become an effective executive.

Strong Will

If those who plan to achieve something keep up steadfastness throughout, they will achieve what they plan.

Kural 666

Some people may have a determined mind to do a task resolutely at the time of launching it. But in the course of performing it, they lose the intensity of their determination. Their mind will lose its firmness. Consequently, they will lose their hold on the task. Such people will fail to achieve anything according to their plans.

The determination and resoluteness of mind should be kept up and maintained until the goal is reached. No wavering. No withdrawing. No slumbering. To keep the mind as if it were cast in steel, straight, not bent or twisted is the secret of various achievements made by the great men of history.

This is not a mere hypothesis. It is a proved psychological fact that anybody can reckon with. This precept is meant not only for the executives but also for all in all walks of life. Once an executive is resolved to accomplish a task, he should not be perturbed by any pediments that may be encountered, he should not loosen his mind so as to become lax in the middle. He should go on and on with the same vigour and vigil until the task is finished.

A clear-visioned executive can forecast well in advance any impediment that may arise in the course of the implementation of a project. He will anticipate them beforehand.

In that case, such impediments will not cause any adverse reaction on his mind.

When you have resolved upon a task, waver not, languish not.
But, pursue and accomplish without slumbering.

Kural 668

Firmness of Action

Avoid ruinous deeds in advance; not to be perturbed by the obstacles that may crop up in the middle—these are the ways to secure the firmness in action as per the maxim of the wise.

Kural 662

'Disaster Control' is a technique applied in advance to minimise the effects of exceedingly unlikely but extremely dangerous threats which if they materialise, would be dangerous in any project.

'Brainstorming' is another technique in which rapid generation of original thoughts are evolved at a meeting specially convened for the purpose at which all present bring up as many ideas as possible on a selected subject without any inhibition.

By this brainstorming process and counseling as necessary, ruinous impediments that may arise in the implementation of a project can be forecast in advance. This will help in avoiding hurdles before their occurrence.

But, in spite of such precautionary steps, some problems may crop up unexpectedly which will threaten the entire project.

There are numerous techniques available in modern management practices by which any eventuality can be met with. One such technique is called 'Damage Control' which is a system of standardised reporting and action-taken/to be taken, combined with a 'motivation campaign' in which all incidents which cause material or property damage apart from production spoilage are highlighted. Reporting of incidents is followed by the appropriate remedial measures. And such reports will be summarised and analysed so that action can be taken over a wider field so as to eliminate or reduce the conditions that will cause the most expensive incidents (damage to the project).

What is to be kept in mind by an effective executive is:
To beware of the ruinous deeds in advance. Not to be perturbed if any such things arise—considered method is this for the resoluteness of action to be upheld and achieved.

Disclose not the Ultimate Purpose

True manliness is to execute and then reveal,
as woes ensue if exposed in the middle.

Kural 663

Success in a big undertaking lies in delegating the major tasks by the chief executive of the concern, so that the disclosure of the ultimate purpose of those tasks coincides with the final fulfillment of the undertaking.

The delegation technique in this way will also help the delegate develop himself.

When delegating a particular job, the delegate should not be told how to do the job. The delegate may be asked to say how he is going to do the job. By so exercising his mind, the delegate will train himself in devising the methods of doing his work by himself in future. But the executive can share information and background material with him. He may also make himself available to answer questions on the spot. If the task that is delegated is quite new, the executive need not assign the whole task at a stretch. He can outline the entire project and leave a part of the project with the delegate and ask him to report when it is completed. Then the executive can evaluate the completed part of the project and delegate the next stage of the project. This is the secret of effective delegation of work and successful completion of the project.

There is a psychological factor also in this respect. It is a fact that if the ultimate purpose of the task is disclosed by the chief executive before the task is accomplished, the resoluteness or the determination of his mind is likely to be loosened. Once the resoluteness is lost, the executive is very unlikely to have the task accomplished as he planned.

Moreover, the premature disclosure of the purpose of a task will cause impediments from unsocial or hostile people who are widespread in modern society. Some delegates may try to exploit the situation with respect to the ultimate purpose of the task if it is known to them in advance.

Delay not over Decision after Deliberation

The end of all deliberation is to arrive at a bold decision.
And it is bad if that decision is kept in cold storage,
in dilatoriness.

Kural 671

Much of the day of a chief executive is spent in acquiring information. They will come quite often through verbal exchanges. The executive has also to be a good listener. He has to ask his subordinates questions, the answers to which will supply the required information and data for the executive to decide the course of action he has to take.

Besides the personal deliberations with his subordinates and competent counsellors, written reports from the subordinates may also be necessitated for the ad hoc data to be validated. It is obvious that the decision-making process depends finally on how well the executive comprehends the facts and issues facing his business. That is why information gathering is very important for any executive. Other activities like conveying information and making decisions are all governed by the gathered information.

After listening to the deliberation and counselling and after gathering the required information and data, the executive must evaluate and think over them deeply and thoroughly, If the decision-making can be done after a few days, and if the executive is not yet ready to make up his mind, he can sleep on it for some time. Let his subconscious mind do a little work. Then the decision should be made. Once a decision is made, that decision should not be kept in cold storage for days together.

It may be hard to act immediately. On many occasions it needs courage; it may not be present either. But, after he has acted, the chief executive might wonder why he had not acted much earlier.

If the executive puts his decision into cold storage without putting it into action, he will lose interest in the project. He will lose his determination and resoluteness. As a result, all the time the executive listened to the deliberation and counseling, all the time he thought over what he had listened to will all prove to be a meaningless waste and such lapses on his part will weaken his capacity as an executive besides making his subordinates frustrated.

Delay, Delay Not

Prolong deliberately those actions that may be delayed. But delay not actions which demand promptness and vigilance.

Kural 672

Decisions have to be taken as to which tasks deserve priority and which fall lower in the line and can wait. Only a few executives are able to sort out the work to do now and later. Decisions of priorities are not based on intelligent analysis alone but it depends on one's courage as well. Courage rather than analysis ultimately dictates identifying the priorities. The courage to assess time and events and the decision as to what really matters urgently and comes first is the executive's only hope of becoming a master of time and events.

There may be some big tasks which are very important and which deserve vigilance and personal attention. But still, they may have to be accomplished at a greater span of time so as to suit the completion of the overall project. Such tasks have also to be handled leisurely and by sleeping over them. This sort of classification of the two types of tasks can be specifically made by using some management techniques like the Critical Path Method or PERT technique.

We reiterate the important precept to be adhered to while planning a project by an effective executive.

Sort out such tasks which demand urgent accomplishments and the ones which need a wider span of time. Make selective delay in the case of the latter deeds, and delay not the former ones. There are some universal guidelines for exercising selective delays, which Thiruvalluvar has framed.

Plant the Seeds in Seasons

The executive can plant the seeds of a project by informing one of his subordinates about it and making him start the work. This is a better use of his limited time than simply making notes by himself.

Begin a Complex Project before the Simple Ones

The executive can put off one-stage projects. It is wiser to take up those with many steps and it is better to use his time to work on them.

Work on the Top Projects rather than the Easy Ones

The executive can put off simple tasks for his less productive times and tackle the projects that truly challenge his capabilities.

Allow Space for Procrastination when Required

Suppose in the morning mail the executive receives a long letter from one of his close friends which he has the impulse to read forthwith. But it is totally irrelevant to the project he is currently working on. Now, instead of reading it he can put it aside and tell himself, 'will read it at lunch time if I have done a good morning's work'. Mostly his morning work would be productive and he can enjoy reading the letter with a sense of satisfaction rather than a sense of guilt.

The Five to be Considered

Consider thoroughly all the five aspects—money, means, time, task and place—and then launch the operation.

Kural 675

Before launching a project, the five aspects that would determine the success and purpose of the project should be thoroughly considered without leaving any shadow of doubt.

Of all the five factors, the availability of fund occupies the first place. As per the detailed estimate, the working cost of the project is arrived at and it should be ensured that the full amount of the estimate is made available duly sanctioned by the government or the competent authority. If the funds thus allotted are not sufficient to cover the entire project, it is not advisable to commence the project works. For, half-finished, a project will not serve any purpose. It will become only a dead storage

The second factor is the means such as the required labour-force, sufficient infrastructure in the organisation, technical know-how and transport facilities etc. that are necessary for implementing the project.

Then comes the time factor. Suitable season that favours the required environment and natural resources like water should be selected for proceeding with the project works. And the available duration from the date of commencement up to the deadline fixed should be duly considered. This span of time will decide the price and the progress of the work and the required money and means which are to be commensurate with the required speed of execution.

The fourth factor is the project itself. The nature of the various tasks in the project, their need of money, means and time has to be considered thoroughly. This will enable the executive to sort out the tasks requiring priority and those that will fall under afterwards.

The fifth factor under consideration is the place of the project. Whether the particular place is suitable for constructing the project with respect to its ultimate purpose; whether the environment of that place will be conducive to going ahead with the project works without any obstacles; whether the socio-economic condition of the people will suit the launching of the project there; and such other aspects will have to be considered.

So, the planning and processing of a project will have to be done by duly considering the five aspects—money, means, task, place and time.

Examine Three Aspects

Judge the mode of completion, hurdles and gain
before you plunge into an action.

Kural 676

First of all, before launching a project, the end in view should be considered, whether the project can be brought to its successful completion with the available resources. Whether a project can be completed within a particular period of time so as to serve a specified purpose and such other factors have to be considered beforehand.

Besides the actual strength and potentialities of the organisation, the executive should also examine in advance, impediments or obstacles that may arise in the course of operation.

The most important prior consideration is over the actual benefits that will accrue from the completion of the task.

It should be ascertained whether the specific purpose for which the particular project is to be undertaken will be served on its accomplishment. Suppose, the project on hand is for construction of hutments or kutcha quarters meant for the tribal people who are habituated to earn their livelihood hunting. It should be thought over and ascertained in advance whether those people who lead a gypsy life will come forward to settle in a particular place and occupy the proposed hutments. After the completion of all the proposed hutments if the gypsy people bluntly refuse to live there, what would be the ultimate result? The very aim of the project will fail utterly and the entire amount spent on the project will go to waste.

Proper Planning

The energy that is spent on actions without proper planning will prove to be failure, whatever man-power is deployed to its successful accomplishment.

Kural 468

Planning is essential for any kind of function. The army commander plans his onslaughts and his retreat with a degree of precision. Even the chief of dacoits proceeds only after careful planning.

Details are important; timing is of essence; required human-power, manager and staff are crucial. Every aspect of the operation will have to be thought over and lived through in advance in imagination and comprehension.

Planning is the searchlight of human wisdom. It helps to foresee the hazards or pitfalls well in time, so that the executive can be equipped to face them when they arise. It also throws light on the possible opportunities and latent potentialities of a situation/person that otherwise may be missed by oversight.

If proper planning is not done in advance, mere striving and hard work or deploying excess manpower will not help to take the project to its successful end. For example, for a successful dry cultivation in the plains in India, it should be planned to plough the land during summer months before cultivation. If summer-ploughing is not planned and carried out, the crops will be overpowered by weeds, and the farmers will have to resort to intensive weeding by deploying more and more labour. However, this will not help, because the sprouting of overwhelming weeds will curtail the growth of crops to a considerable extent.

Hence, the successful accomplishment of any task mainly rests on proper planning. In order to make well-defined planning, deliberations with a body of tried counsellors will be imperative. The administrator should prefer to have around him the ablest and trusted people. He can also seek the counsel of his peers from other sister organisations and of enlightened people from among the public also, who will be in a position to give some important practical tips. Such deliberations will help the executive or administrator decide the wastage, the output and the ultimate gain that the project would yield.

There are things that ought to be delayed, as progress or the purpose of the scheme itself may be spoiled. And there are some urgent things that ought to be done at any cost.

Kural 466

Such and other factors can be considered thoroughly during the deliberations to be held beforehand.

Nothing is hard for him who acts after deliberation with a body of tried and well known counselors.

Kural 462

A well-qualified person with higher education alone cannot be expected to possess the required know-how in any task.

Even on the part of those who possess the rarely available higher education qualifications devoid of any faults, lack of ignorance is rare.

Kural 503

Counseling is the technique by which an experienced person gives advice on the problem at hand, or on the intrinsic details of the task with which the executive is entrusted.

In performance of a task, the executive has to know the intrinsic details of its operation from experts having intimate knowledge of the task.

Kural 677

A case study may be made for understanding the various details of the work as experienced by a typical person. It is a learning technique in which the real situation or a case study of actual events is presented to the learner (either orally or on paper) for his analysis and consideration of possible solution to the various problems identified in a task.

Whatever method is adopted, the aim of the executive should be to learn the intrinsic details thoroughly, so as to do proper planning before he launches any project.

Proceed on any task after careful deliberation and comprehension. He is a fool who steps into action first and says that he would think over it afterwards.

Kural 467

Two Mangoes with a Single Stone

As one elephant is used for capturing another one, so one action can be utilised in having another one accomplished.

Kural 678

'With a single stone, strike two mangoes' is a proverb in Tamil. There are numerous examples that can be quoted to highlight this aspect. In the 'On Farm Development' work, the executive constructs a field channel for irrigating. The same irrigation channel will be made to as drainage channel as well in suitable topography as in Kuttanadu and Java. Here, the task of constructing a separate drainage channel is accomplished in the design of constructing an irrigation channel.

Effectiveness in Meetings

An effective executive will conduct periodical meetings to review the progress of the various projects under his control. He will also have to conduct some process-oriented special meetings, whenever some special purpose demands. An effective executive, with a sense of time-consciousness, will utilise the periodical meetings for accomplishing the purpose of a special meeting too.

Thus an executive can increase his leverage in executing his works; the output of an executive is the output of his organisation.

In principle, more money, more manpower or more facilities can always be made available, but our own time is the one absolute finite resource. How one handles time is the most important aspect on his part for being a role model or a leader. Meetings provide occasion for managerial activities. Getting together with others is a medium; the executive can do his work in a meeting, in a memo etc. But he must choose the most effective medium for what he wants to accomplish, and that gives him the greatest leverage.

Leverage of managerial activity is the measure of the output generated by the individual members of the organisation.

Hence, Managerial output = Output of the organisation
= L X A + L2 X A2 + • • • •
Where L = Leverage
A = Member of the organisation.

A manager/executive's output is thus the result of the individuals activities having varying degree of leverage. It is clear that the key to high output means being sensitive to the leverage of what the executive does during the day.

Managerial productivity, the output per unit time can be increased in three ways:

i) Increasing the rate of performing his activities, speeding up his works.

ii) Increasing the leverage associated with the various managerial activities.

iii) Shifting from those with lower leverage to those with higher leverage.

High leverage activities are done

1) When many people are affected by one manager.

2) When a person's activities or behaviour over a long period of time is affected by a manager's brief, well-focused actions.

An effective executive will be an expert in time-management. And effective time management will mean maintaining a high degree of the executive's leverage on whatever task he may undertake which includes his making each of his actions in accomplishing another one or more and in training his whole organisation to this effect.

Action Through Feasible Ways

Action through all feasible ways is good. If there is no such way ahead of him, let him proceed on the possible line of least resistance.

Kural 673

Anyone who intends to lead a full-fledged life has to go on working through all possible ways. 'Work is worship' is a saying that has sprung from well-established human practice. Continued actions produce not only continuous gains but they also help the actionist (doer) develope step by step with more and more experience to his credit. Action breeds actions. An actionist activates himself and also others. He will willingly undertake a multitude of actions.

He who toils tirelessly will overcome the unfavourable nature. Such is the power of the vibrant actionist.

Kural 620

The actionists alone are they who are alive in this world in a real sense. All the others simply follow the actionists for their bread.

In primitive society, some excelled as warriors, some as hunters, and some as fishermen. And in each function, individuals varied somewhat but the number and scope of functions were limited. Today, the general category of jobs number tens or hundreds or thousands while the sub-categories are many times as numerous, and each one of successive incumbents in a single post will handle his/her responsibilities in his/her own way.

As such, the scope of individuality is enormously widened even though the superficial appearances may seem to standardise the man.

Most of the production practices follow well established procedures and use specific methods that have been found feasible. But, sometimes, even such methods may be stuck due to unforeseen circumstances. The executive, on some occasions, has to rise to the occasion with an instantaneous decision to follow some other methods which will possibly lead him to success.

An executive is mainly an actionist. Action through all feasible ways is good. If there is no such way ahead, let him choose any other way that will lead him to succeed.

Time Management

A well timed action is the sure cord
that binds the fortune indeed.

Kural 482

An effective executive will always keep in his mind that time is his one finite resource, and that appropriate time and season is an important factor for carrying out any project. He has to be an expert in managing the time when he says 'Yes' to one thing and he says an emphatic 'no' to another.

The medium of the executive's forecast is his calendar. In order to have better control of his time, the executive should use his calendar as a production 'planning tool', taking a firm initiative to schedule his work that is not time-critical between those 'limiting steps' in the day.

To use his calendar as a production planning tool, he must accept responsibility for the following two things:

- He should move towards the active use of his calendar, taking the initiative to fill the holes between the time critical events with the non-time critical ones, though these are necessary activities.
- He should say 'no' at the outset to work beyond his capacity to handle.

Effective Managerial Performance

An executive or a manager cannot hide himself for fear of interruptions. He has to be receptive to anybody who wants to see him. He must understand that the interrupters may be having some legitimate problems that make them approach him. But the executive can channelise the time needed to deal with them into organised schedules by providing a fixed time for 'meeting' them.

The point is to impose a pattern on the manner manager copes with problems. To make something regular that was once irregular is a fundamental managerial principle. Only by adhering to this principle, a manager can conserve the available time favourable for a particular task or project and make use of it effectively.

Nothing is impossible for the executive if he keeps the favourable season effectively under his disposal and orients his task well to suit the season, with the required means, of course.

Kural 483

Agricultural operations are a concrete example for the season-orienting principle. Similarly, construction of buildings or massive dams have to be taken up only during a season when conditions are favourable.

When a rare and ripe season arises one can dare to do rare things.

Kural 489

Hence one should be vigilant and watchful over the coming and going of seasonal environments. And the executive should be ready to strike the very opportune occasion for accomplishing the rarely possible things.

This sort of conduct is just like the stork patiently awaiting a delicious fish to come along and pecking it when it comes.

Kural 490

If the opportune time has not yet come, it will be advisable for the executive to contain himself with all his feelings of urgency to accomplish the task. And if opportune time comes, he can choose even some additional tasks apart from the one on hand to accomplish by making use of such favourable time.

Sense of Fulfillment

Possession of zeal alone is everlasting wealth.
Material possessions are fleeting wealth.

Kural 591

The length of stem of lotus is actually the depth of water holding the flower. The greatness of a man is similarly as much as the elevation of his mind.

Kural 595

Mental elevation is true manhood. Lacking it, man is like a mere wood.

Hence, the precept of 'Valluvam' for a high-level executive or an administrator is to have an elevated mind with a sense of pride. Such a man will be able to do mighty deeds for the betterment of the organisation and to society at large. An effective executive derives his actual strength only by virtue of strength of his organisation, even though he himself has to act as a role model. Organisational strength is nothing but the strength of its constituent members. The administrator should therefore find ways and means to build up the organisational strength by building up his team members to high caliber.

Motivation

Providing monetary incentive is one of the ways of increasing the capacity of the employees. Incentive can also be provided by non-monetary factors. Recognition of personal dignity and importance will be an effective incentive for anyone.

The theory of motivation by Abraham Maslow is based on psychology of human behaviour. For Maslow, motivation is closely connected with the needs which cause people to respond positively. A need once satisfied ends the source of motivation. Hence, if a higher degree of motivation is to be created and maintained, some higher-needs have to be identified that will need motivation all along.

Maslow defined a set of needs that tend to lie in a hierarchy. When a lower need is satisfied, a higher need is likely to take over its place. The physiological needs, safety or security, and also social needs can motivate people for better work. But other higher needs like self-esteem and self-actualisation will act as more effective and perennial motivational forces.

Self Actualisation

For Maslow, self-actualisation stems from a personal realisation—what 'I can do, I must be'. If one's source of motivation is self-actualisation, his drive to perform will have no limits. Thus, its most important characteristic is that, unlike other sources of motivation which extinct after the needs are fulfilled, self-actualisation continues to motivate people to higher and higher level of performance.

The administration needs to create an environment to foster the motivation through self-actualisation among the members of the organisation. For this purpose, objectives may be set at a point so high that even if the individuals push themselves hard, they will still have a fifty-fifty chance of making them. But the total output will tend to go higher and higher since everybody will strive for a higher level of achievement. Such a goal-setting is extremely important if what an executive wants is peak-performance from himself and his subordinates.

All the staff will have to be persuaded and motivated psychologically. They may be trained psychologically and the fact impressed upon them that each one of them has immense power and capacity to achieve anything and everything, provided they begin to tap their limitless mental resources. Thus, they may charge their mind with power by means of self-communication with their heart and mind.

This way of motivating the members of an organisation will instill into their mind what is known as self-actualisation or a sense of self-esteem and pride which will be a permanent motivating factor not only in official discharge of their duties but in elevating their own self-standard in social life. This self-actualisation will not breed egoism or other negative characteristics in one's social life. On the contrary, it will instill only the good qualities like modesty, freedom from insolence etc.

Have it in Mind

It is easy to achieve anything one desires
if he keeps it in his mind, well set.

Kural 540

It is again reiteration of the concept of tapping mental power for achieving things. If one aspires to achieve a particular thing officially or personally, he should go on thinking over it again and again deeply and forcefully so that a deep impression is made on the mind—as a perception that such and such a job can be done or such a thing should be achieved. Intercepting the favourable ways and means, making good the shortcomings or obstacles that may arise in his ways, the favourable means that can be secured for achieving it etc. would be possible by perception, provided the mind is always set at it.

By keeping the desired thing always in his active mind, one becomes a part of it and finds some suitable channels to achieve it. The active mind has such a potential. In order to secure the capacity to achieve a particular thing, what the executive ought to do is to keep the desired thing always in his active mind. It will generate enormous power in his mind which can be tapped by him for the accomplishment of his goal. Hence all the varied activities and responsibilities of the executive should be centered around his goal, firmly set in his mind.

Delegation

THE LARGER an organisation grows, the more important it becomes to delegate work to the various categories of staff in the organisation. By retaining only the personal element in management, each member of the organisation has to be given the feeling that he is having his share of involvement in the affair of the organisation. This can be achieved only by proper delegation throughout the whole length of the administrative chain. To delegate is to give the delegate a sense of responsibility, a feeling of being involved and trusted. Proper delegation of works among all the members of an organisation will give the whole institution a fresh momentum and flexibility.

Many administrators follow the 'do-it-myself' policy. This will result in poor management of time. The subordinates will become bored and sometimes frustrated and may get the impression that the administrator does not have confidence in them. And the administrator will become popular as an easy boss who takes up all the subordinates' work himself. The result will be that the administrator will get confined under a pile of work while his subordinates are without a full day's work.

When the administrator delegates work properly, it will give him more and more working time. It will help him eliminate, pass on, or at least minimise the time-consuming routine jobs that will keep him from his primary duties.

But delegation is not a once-for-all handing over. It involves a continued and maturing relationship between the one who delegates and the other who receives the delegated powers,—which, by its nature, presupposes a willingness to let the other man run the affair in his own way, consistent with his belief, and to stand behind him when he needs support. By the same token, it presupposes the right to call him to account when there has been a serious failure of judgment or a disregard of the basic aims and principles.

Willingness to delegate is one of the characteristics of leadership, as important as any other qualities required for the people in position and authority. 'What is worth doing is worth the trouble of asking somebody to do it.'

Delegation will help the administrator upgrade his subordinates and mould them as capable executives. Their enhanced competence can then be better utilised in other development work. Thus, delegation multiplies results.

In the administrative climate of the modern world, it is essential to develop shared executive skills. Formerly most part of an administration could be understood and handled by one single person. But now, with computers, day to day complex problems and growing government regulations, a smart administrator allows specialists to handle their areas of expertise, thereby freeing him to concentrate on his own job of administering. The administrator must realise that planning functions have to be kept as his own responsibility and operating and all other functions must be delegated to others.

The key to delegation is closeness, which breeds a team spirit. The delegator should take time to learn about his subordinates, study them and assess their capabilities as well as their conduct and character. Delegation should be based only on this assessment.

This part of the book deals with basic aspects of assessing the subordinates for effective delegation. It has to be remembered that Thiruvalluvar rendered these basic concepts 2,000 years ago.

Choose Right People

> *After ascertaining with care that 'this man would accomplish this job with this particular means', the responsibility of doing it should be left to him.*
>
> Kural 517

Everybody in this world is unique in fingerprint, in personality and other features. That no one is exactly duplicated means every person has some values that signify rarity. Individuality accords everyone a particular place in society. At the same time, anyone and everyone has limitations in point of view, skills and experience. The advance of civilisation is a long march in the direction of further differentiating people, making all persons more and more different from each other in knowledge, background and skills.

As such, an administrator has to study each and every man under his control and learn about him thoroughly.

The administrator can thus prepare a chart in which the individuals' special educational qualifications, skills, knowledge and experience are noted clearly. The allocation of work already made to each individual and the time taken by him to complete the work can be noted against his name in the chart. This chart will help the administrator determine the most suitable candidate for a particular job.

Utmost care should be exercised in ascertaining that a particular individual, if provided with particular means, can accomplish a particular job.

Productivity of human resources requires people with potential, skill and knowledge. Assignment control is the key to the productivity of the skilled worker.

This requires, first, that the administrator should know the strength of his people and particularly of those with a proven record of performance. He may ask himself:'What do they do well? Where do they belong?' It requires, secondly, that as far as possible people are assigned where the application of their strength will produce results. A particular individual may satisfy with regard to his good physique, mental energy, good conduct etc. but, when the question of accomplishing a particular task arises, he may differ adversely. That is to say,

An individual may pass every kind of test but still he may fail when the responsibilities of accomplishing a particular task is entrusted to him.

Kural 514

Freedom to Subordinates

Once a particular subordinate is fixed for a particular task, transfer to him full responsibility and authority to do it.

Kural 518

No holder of a task can ever achieve it unless he is provided with the means to do it. The means is, of course, the authority and necessary power to do the task.

If the means are wider than the ends, part of it will go to waste or may be misused, but, if it is narrower, adequacy will be lacking and the ends cannot be possibly achieved. The means must therefore match the ends; authority and the task, results and accountability must go together.

Conferring the delegate with the required authority commensurate with the responsibility is essential for him to accomplish the task effectively. Then only, other men who are supposed to assist the delegate in carrying out the job, will respond to his command and cooperate with him with due seriousness.

It is natural that an administrator may expect his people to adopt his own methods and procedures in carrying out the jobs. But the administrator must understand that the individual human being who is at work knows better than anybody else what makes him more productive and what is helpful or unhelpful to him.

It requires acceptance of the fact that the person who does the job is likely to know more about the job than the administrator. He may prefer to follow his own methods; the delegate must therefore be given freedom to procede by himself.

The best way to make sure that delegation is effective is to stress on the results rather than the methods.

'The best executive is one who has sense enough to pick a good man to do what he wants him to do and restrain enough to keep from meddling with him while he does it.' (Attributed to Theodore Roosevelt.)

Worldly Wisdom

Don't look down upon any person on the face of his unimpressive figure, for there are men like the axle-pin of the mighty rolling car.

Kural 667

Classification of the subordinate into two extremities as clever-dull, efficient-inefficient, capable-incapable, good-bad and so on, and labelling them according to such opinions formed in the mind of the administrator need not be always correct. Formation of such extreme opinions and delegating jobs based on them will leave many men without adequate work and burden the chosen few with all the tough jobs. Ultimately, it will prove to be a poor delegation. It will result in non-utilisation of the available manpower to its full capacity while rendering many people with a feeling of frustration, of being either undervalued or overburdened.

Every person is a unique individual with special skill or traditionally inherent potential. The central feature of a good administration is to contribute to the development of all the members of the organisation, irrespective of their qualification, experience, impressive features or otherwise.

The only way by which the burden of administration in advancing civilisations can be made manageable is by enhancing the capacity and utilising the knowledge and potential of all the subordinates.

The administrator would do well if he takes time to impart job-training to his people in areas they are not familiar with. Such training and development of the constituents of an organisation will yield multiple results.

Nobody in any organisation can be declared as fit for nothing. Everybody will be having his own characteristics and capabilities. Even the basic servants, now known as Office Assistants, will be able to take initiative in many of the office-routines which the other staff may not be in a position to perform. Hence no individual should be ignored as insignificant.

A man may fail miserably in his private business in which his individual initiative will be the main criterion for success. But the same person, if employed in a public scheme, may even excel others in carrying out his duties under proper guidance by a high level administrator.

Similarly, some executives may find it difficult to work as one among numerous executives under an administrative head, but the same person, if entrusted to hold the responsibility of implementing a scheme, may prove to be a successful executive. And also, the vice-versa will be the case with many other executives.

Don't we know the following nursery rhyme, Worldly Wise?

For want of a nail
The shoe was lost,
For want of a shoe
The horse was lost
For want of a horse
The rider was lost
For want of a rider
The battle was lost
For want of a battle
The kingdom was lost
And all for the want
Of a horse shoe nail

Here, the 'worldly wisdom' is that even a horse shoe nail should not be undervalued. Even a tiny piece of wood will be useful for cleaning the teeth. Hence the precept of Valluvam: *Despise not men of modest appearance. Don't you know of such men who are like the axle-pin of a mighty rolling car?*

Assess the Traits

Trust that man who possesses an enduring love,
discriminating knowledge, clarity of mind and
non-craving for property.

Kural 513

One of the findings of a psychological research on personality and performance has disclosed, among other things, that personality test-scores have higher validity than interview rating or performance tests and that personality or character traits are much more important than even the possession of skills in the discharge of duties.

i) Top rated supervisors find it easy to get along with their men due to their even-tempered, consistent and friendly manners, whereas: the low rated supervisors are nervous and either too withdrawn or too aggressive. *Love is the most important aspect in human personality.*

If one does not have this aspect in his heart,
all other parts of his body will prove to be in vain.

Kural 79

Love breeds considerateness which is essential for a positive human behaviour in dealing with peers and subordinates.

ii) Individual differences in linguistic habits cause difference in the ability to solve problems such as sorting and discrimination. The effective solution of problems necessitates knowledge. Men of knowledge will foresee the outcome of their actions and anticipate the intruding problems before they actually arise, and hence, they are well-poised for taking up any assignment. The productivity of the people requires continuous learning, as the Japanese are doing. It requires that people are constantly challenged to think over as to what they can do to improve what they are already doing. It requires adoption of the specific Japanese Zen concept of learning: 'One learns in order to do better what one already knows how to do well'.

iii) Clarity of mind goes with sharp intellect. People with sharp intellect will not dilly-dally whenever instantaneous decisions have to be made at times when serious problems crop up against the progress of a scheme.

iv) The fourth factor necessary for a trustworthy supervisor is non-craving for property. With all the people in public administration, this factor must be essentially inherent which will help them develop a dedicated service to the public. Coveting public property is a social crime. Hence such men in public administration, who are inclined to coveting public property, should not be considered trustworthy on any other counts. They should be regarded as weeds to be either removed or isolated and kept under continuous vigil.

Test and Trust

To trust anybody without test, to doubt subsequently the trusted will both entail troubles that will last long.

Kural 510

For trusting a person to delegate a task to him, there are two ways of looking at it. Do not trust anyone until he proves he deserves it, or, trust him to do his best until he proves otherwise. The second may be more applicable in public administration. But still, it is better to have some idea of the individual in question and of his capabilities. This can be a high risk policy and occasionally it may go wrong. But if the administrator is a good judge, he will not make mistakes.

The most important thing for an administrator is to study his men and anticipate how they may react in given circumstances. Nobody in any organisation can be expected to be perfect in all respects. But each individual should be studied and assessed with respect to requirements. His integrity, his working knowledge, intelligence, non-craving for public property and such other basic qualities have to be assessed and the administrator has to be satisfied before selecting him for carrying out a particular task.

It may become immensely dangerous to trust anybody without testing him sufficiently.

But, after trusting a subordinate and delegating an important task to him, if the administrator begins to doubt him, then again the administrator will be in trouble. 'Delegate and forget' is a blind management policy. But, if the administrator develops doubt in his mind about the person after delegating a task to him, he is not yet freed himself from the burden of the task, but actually he is overburdening himself by doubting the delegate.

Hence the precept. Not to trust anybody without testing him sufficiently and, once an individual is trusted, not to doubt him subsequently without cause is the best policy in management philosophy.

Choose not anybody without proper examination, and once you have selected somebody, find out appropriate jobs for him to accomplish.

Kural 509

If the administrator has once selected a person for the executive post, he should not hold him under distrust.

Trust begets trust and mistrust begets mistrust.

Only if the employee feels that he is a trusted person in the organisation, he will be in a position to work freely with self-confidence. But if he is made to feel that he is not trusted by his superior, he will lose his self-confidence and will not try to build himself by self-initiative. The very feeling that he is doubted by his superior will make him feel frustrated, suppressed and curtailed. He will hesitatingly refer to his superior at every moment of his discharging his duty without adequate necessity because of the lack of self-confidence. As such, the organisation cannot expect him to work to his full capacity.

Choosing the Executives

THE STRENGTH of an organisation rests in its constituent members. There are many instances whercin an excellent organisation has gone down with decay in leadership and management, and conversely, a sick organisation has acquired a new lease of life merely by the change of a few key persons in the organisation,

With each new entrant, brick by brick, the executive edifice of the organisation is either strengthened or eroded. An executive does not bring in a mere skill or talent; he brings with him a personality, fervour, a nuance that surrounds him as an atmosphere. He can exude fragrance or stench that infuses or infects others in the team. He is always a force.

Selection of executives will have to be made according to the culture or tradition of the organisation and the nature and significance of the assignment. Certain empirical suggestions can be made for the selection of personnel for the posts.

i) Where a new and sophisticated department is opened, say, a computer department, and in the case of a professional and skilled function, new blood and fresh outlook may be injected. Outsiders with special skills may be considered.
ii) In a few other disciplines, both internal and external aspirants can be considered.
iii) For the large body of routine functions at relatively lower levels, the general rule should be to select from among the internal candidates. There is also an organisational compulsion to maintain this policy so as to keep the morale of the existing employees and also to prevent waves of inferiority complex, frustration aid conflict from engulfing them.

The corollary of this third policy would be to evaluate systematically and classify the existing employees into four categories:

1	Asset	immediately promotable
2	Satisfactory	promotable in due course
3	Not satisfactory	to be retained and further watched
4	A liability	to be separated

Here, in this part of the book, the basic traits and desirable conduct of the aspirants for the post of executive as laid down by Valluvam are shown and expounded. These basic factors are applicable to both public administration and private concerns.

Assess the Goodness

Look to the good character on the one hand and the evil on the other, assess which of the two predominates and then make your selection accordingly.

Kural 504

Nobody in this world can be expected to be ideal or perfect, possessing only good traits and positive factors. One's traits are developed based on the environment and the family background in which he has been brought up, the institution in which he studied, his psychological makeup etc.

A person can be properly understood and trusted by testing him on the strength of his inclinations or virtue, pleasure and fear of life.

Kural 501

Whatever may be one's educational or other enrichment, his realness or meanness will be decided only by the touchstone of his deeds or his conduct which is shaped by his actions.

Kural 505

Besides many positive factors, an individual may possess some undesirable traits like short temper, anger, selfishness and disregard for the superiors. Assessment has to be made as to how much his positive traits will be helpful to the organisational goal and also how far his negative character will go against the morale of the organisation. Evaluation of the net worth will help the administrator in deciding whether the aspirant for the post is worth or not.

Some good characteristics may be marked in an individual who will offset the other undesirable factors in him. Hence the assessment of the eligibility or otherwise of an individual has to be made only with respect to his positive utility to the organisation. If one's integrity is beyond dispute, his lack of experience or working knowledge need not stand in the way of his eligibility for a post. He can be suitably trained and helped to gain knowledge and experience.

Whom To Trust?

The man born of a good family, having the sensitivity of shame, being free from criminal defects and who shrinks from deeds of disgrace can well be trusted.

Kural 502

The type of family in which a person is born and brought up is mostly responsible for his inherent character and psychological makeup. It is the family which provides the environment for a person to build his personality and inherit the basic traits. If a man comes from a notorious criminal family, he is likely to inherit a criminal bent of mind. In any society there are numerous examples that can be quoted in support of this social finding.

Exceptionally there are many instances where personalities are built up by surroundings, conscientious attitudes and innovative motivation. Circumstances become more powerful than DNA. It should be noted that Thiruvalluvar does not give any special place to the birth of an individual.

Tho' human beings in their birth are the same,
by diverse trade their worth isn't the same.

Kural 972

And, as to sensitivity of shame, non-existence of serious defects and being ashamed of disgrace, they will all follow suit with the background of one's own upbringing.

Hence, before trusting anybody, find out the background of the family in which he was born and brought up. If it's good that man would be sensitive to public censure and free from defects, you can be assured.

Avoid one lacking Social Bondage

Avoid choosing a man who is not having any family or social bondage and who, devoid of any attachment, would not feel shy of any sin.

Kural 506

Human beings are social animals. Every man brought up by the family in which he was born and the society to which he belongs is tied with a human bondage with reference to his family and the society. The stimuli for all his actions and reactions are provided by the family and the society. He will orient all his actions and behaviour towards his social attachment. He will feel ashamed of any indulgence to the detriment of his social prestige.

Conversely, if a man does not have any virtue, social bondage or obligation, he may not hesitate to do anything. He will not be in a position to receive any stimuli from the society so as to streamline his conduct towards goodness.

If such a man is selected as an executive, he cannot be expected to show any seriousness to safeguard the name of the organisation. He may lack in his loyalty to the organisation. He may not hesitate to do anything against its prestige, in the absence of any human bondage, he will not be having any sensitivity to shame, he won't mind doing deeds of disgrace and will not fear public censure. He may indulge in actions against the organisation.

Care should be taken to avoid such a man from entering the organisation.

Objectivity in Selection

Do not choose a man who is not possessing required knowledge for the post of an executive, out of mere fondness, this will result in folly.

Kural 507

While selecting for the post of an executive, the administrator must exercise care and sense of duty and responsibility and not any fondness or favouritism. The aspirants should be studied in depth and assessed dispassionately. Whether the desirable qualities are found with a particular aspirant: what is his potentiality, what is his background, what is his outlook in life and such other factors should be thoroughly studied in order to find out whether he is fit for the post.

But, without any sense of responsibility, by mere fondness

or love or affection, if the administrator selects anybody for a responsible executive post, a chain of undesirable and harmful effects can follow:

- The administrator himself will not be in a position to extract work from such a favourite employee.
- The employee may not show any seriousness in learning things and discharging his assigned duties.

The superior officer to whom this employee is directly answerable will find it difficult to have sufficient control over him because of his awareness that this individual is the man of the administrator.

The colleagues and peers of this man will develop a feeling of frustration because he is shown undue favouritism.

As a consequence of all these factors, the morale of the organisation will get spoiled.

If favouritism, fondness and partisan attitude are shown by the administrator continuously in selecting men for the various posts under his control, the line of control in the official hierarchy will be twisted, which means that the administration has become poor.

Hence personal fondness should not find place in the selection of men for any executive post. Whether the aspirant has working knowledge of the jobs or an inclination to learn things so as to cope up with the ever-changing and ever-increasing activities of the executive are the aspects which have to be mainly assessed.

Beware of the Despicable

What is the base fit for? When occasion arises they are bound to sell themselves fast ignoring loss of face.

Kural 1080

One method of classifying people either outside or within an organisation places them into three groups: the Fits, the Misfits and the Counterfeits. If we consider these three categories within an organisation, the Fits in the first group give the administrator little trouble. They adjust satisfactorily to their jobs and to their colleagues and make the administrative head wish that all employees were like them. They are real assets for the organisation as well as to the nation. But the second category, the Misfits will find it difficult to adjust and will involuntarily create difficulties for the organisation and to themselves. They will require considerable attention by their controlling officers so that they may be corrected and developed as satisfactory producers.

And finally comes the third category, the Counterfeits, a few of whom can be found in any organisation. They are the people who make no effort to adjust to the work situation, who go along simply for the ride, who deliberately create disturbance, and who are incorrigible. They cannot be altered. It will be a very time-consuming and costly affair to reclaim them if the organisation so desires.

One facet of effective human relations involves the ability to detect the differences between the misfits who deserve sympathy, help, guidance and consideration and the counterfeits who deserve no consideration. If the third category of the counterfeits are the aspirants for selection for any post, the administrator should be careful enough not to select them on any consideration. And if they are already employees in an organisation, they must either be dropped if possible, or such persons should be isolated and kept under close observation and continuous vigil.

Thiruvalluvar describes the various facets of these counterfeits, the mean, the base or the despicable.

The mean seem to look like all other people in their form. Such a similarity we have not come across.

Kural 1071

More blessed are the bases than the men of conscience, for they have no pangs of the heart for good or bad.

Kural 1072

The conduct of the mean is based on fear; what would they have? Some desire, posing discipline.

Kural 1075

The base are like the tom-tom, for they speak out to others deliberately every secret they hear.

Kural 1076

Good men would serve at the mere words of direction. But the base can be put to use only by crushing them like sugarcane.

Kural 1078

Every society has to be cautious with the despicable. And particularly the administrator should take every care not to admit such people into the organisation, for, their involvement in the organisation would prove to be dangerous. But in the modern world, the entrance of these incorrigible men of no worth into the arena of public administration cannot be completely arrested. However, if the administration is alert and vigilant enough, the despicable can be conveniently separated, isolated and kept under close observation.

The caution for the administrators is: Beware of the despicable. They will not have any hesitation in betraying the organisation, if they are likely to have some personal benefits, if the ripe occasion arises, they will resort to strike the sales deed for selling anything and everything including self.

Leadership and Personnel Management

IN ANY administrative system, leadership plays the most vital role. Every institution needs a leading individual not merely to see that it carries out its functions on the lines laid down with the object of implementing the policy, but also to provide it with inspiration to develop and maintain its morale. Effective leadership is much more than the mere giving of orders. As a matter of fact, it must emanate from the persons with wide sympathies and a broad cultural viewpoint. Its greatest virtue is enthusiasm. Leadership without enthusiasm, however well conceived is inevitably something less than the best.

Leaders stand out by being different. They question assumptions and are suspicious of tradition. They seek out the truth and make decisions based on fact, not prejudice. They have a preference for innovation.

Leaders are observant and sensitive to people. They know their team and develop mutual confidence within.

They state clear objectives and encourage a sense of security by defining the territory for individual action. They delegate real authority and do not interfere. They praise rather than criticise.

They are humble rather than dogmatic, humorous rather than earnest, diffident rather than overbearing. They encourage initiative and ensure that success is recognised and rewarded. They are followed not only with respect but with a sense of curiosity and even affection. They make life enjoyable for their team by the promise of surprise, excitement, and above all, of solid achievement.

As for personnel management, it is an art in which an effective leader is well versed. Communication, consultation, delegation, managing groups, inter-personal relationships, selection, promotion etc. are some of the aspects of personnel management.

Personal relationships that the administrative leader should inculcate in his staff are the characteristics of a leading executive. Thiruvalluvar indicates the methods by which an executive leader should deal with his staff in order to make himself more and more effective as an executive.

Administer Justice with Rectitude

With thoughtful consideration test and attest impartially; consult and enforce the law justly—this is the way to administer properly.

Kural 541

An administrative head in a large organisation should be effective with all his staff. He has to exercise skills in avoiding personal offence. He must be knowing how and when to appease and persuade his subordinates by using his quick emotional perception.

He should not subscribe to any cliques or groups. He must be impersonal and fair towards individuals. He has also to be considerate and defensive of his subordinates. That is to say, he has to have no favourites, nor cronies, but respond to special opportunities to be helpful.

In any organisation, there occurs the evil of groups among employees due to intrusion of some vested interests. If the administrator favours any one group, the morale of the organisation will get spoilt and the administration will become ineffective. He will also lose his administrative leverage. His words of authority, his directions and his management will get diluted and lose their mettle. In short, he will become a poor administrator.

Impartiality is a jewel adorning an administrator of supreme power and helps him remain well-poised like the weighing balance so as to look to all his staff with equity, to test and attest them without bias and to exercise his authority judiciously.

Ups and downs, or, the loss and gain in terms of accomplishment of duties and responsibilities will be there in any administration but the administrator should be straight and unbent in his entire zone of authority,

A thoughtless tyrant will lose
both his wealth and citizens.

Kural 554

While being effective with his people, the administrator should avoid using his power and authority for his own personal profit; but use them readily when his responsibility demands, he will have to keep his power in reserve, available for exceptional occasions. Such a judicious application of his power will not only make the administrator more and more effective, it will also make his people to look at him with respect, with a sense of curiosity and admiration.

Have a Benign Outlook

Benign look is truly the way of life on earth.
Men sans mercy are burden to earth.

Kural 572

The important quality in human relations is to be considerate and to give recognition to others. Warmheartedness and considerateness are the traits that can be acquired. The best way to do this is by going through the motions, for, as one psychologist has said, by this, one will tend to acquire the corresponding emotions. This holds good more in the case of administrators.

Considerateness involves first in using the names of the individuals while calling them and conversing with them.

Chatting with them now and then, criticising only in private, praising them in the presence of others and discussing with them about matters of mutual interest will all go a long way in building up a cordial relationship with them and motivating them for better performance besides helping the administrator in developing the trait of considerateness.

In understanding human nature, it is of basic importance for the administrator to look beyond the surface and realise that performance and attitude may be greatly affected by the personal life of the individual. It is easy to criticise and condemn inadequacies; but judgments can be less harsh and the treatment of the unsatisfactory situations can be handled with more understanding and tact. Knowing the true causes for the defects will help in dealing more effectively with human situations.

In the analysis of a democracy, the citizens, citizen groups, political parties, political leaders, civil servants, technicians and administrators, administrative leaders and workers of many kinds and levels will all form the complementary elements. They are all interdependent features of the organic whole which is a democratic government. Hence it is not difficult to understand that the 'benign outlook' of an administrator will spread to all his staff which, in turn, will be reflected to the people. The civil administrators should always keep it in mind that they are representing the people, though to a much lesser degree than the political administrators.

For such an administrator who would be gracious and considerate to all his people without detriment to his duties, his administrative territory would become his rightful place.

Kural 578

Deal with people benignly. According to Thiruvalluvar, this is the best punishment for the offenders who have done harms.

Punish those who have done great evils
by shaming them with good deeds.

Kural 314

The public administrator will not be able to get the results he wants by enforcing the general staff regulations unless he has a sympathetic understanding of his staff, together with an awareness of the probable impact of his own activities.

Every worker has a right to his private life, and the administrator, in turn, has to understand that the personal troubles of any of his staff will adversely affect the public work. Hence, it is the real essence of the art of administration that the administrator should be able to ease out such troubles without overstepping his legitimate bounds.

The encouragement of social, cultural, and sports activities which are fostered in many branches of public services do go a long way in easing out the stress and strain of individuals' personal problems and in maintaining good humour required in public service.

Only if the administrative leader harbours compassion in his eyes, he will be in a position to deal with all his staff with kindness, ease out their stress and strain, and care for their personal welfare and make them follow his directions wholeheartedly.

What are the tuning chords for, if not accordant with the song?
Of what avail are the eyes not possessing the benign grace?

Kural 573

Grasp the Fruits of Words

The characteristic of the men of spotless worth is to utter attractive words and to grasp the fruits of words from others.

Kural 646

The administrator has to be considerate with benign outlook towards all his staff. He should develop such a trait by himself, and use sweet words on all occasions while conversing with his staff.

Sweet words will always yield good results and lead to administrative virtue. But still, some administrators hold an unfortunate notion that a man of strong authority is one who wields the heaviest whip and sharpest tongue, using only harsh words and sometimes even unparliamentry words. Such a style of functioning will not yield any positive results.

It is just like preferring raw fruits to the ripened
ones while both are available side by side.

Kural 100

Whenever the administrator talks to his subordinates, he should speak in an impressive manner by using sweet words.

At the same time, he should not go on talking without allowing his staff a turn to have their say. He should also cultivate the habit of listening to his staff to the maximum possible extent.

The staff should be consulted on all the matters affecting them. In small organisations or offices, such a discussion is usually informal and spontaneous. In larger organisations like the Directorate of Agriculture, a definite mechanism has to be devised.

Trade union activities have been classified as an external aspect of personnel management, but nevertheless, it is a matter that will have a continuous internal impact and no administrator can act without taking it into active consideration. Besides the staff's union, in the case of larger organisations, a joint council consisting of officials and representative of the staff unions needs to be instituted.

Not only effectiveness of the organisation is increased by the achievement of maximum understanding between the administrator and his staff through a system of joint councils but also the staff having special experience and knowledge can be tapped for the betterment of the organisation. Usually this process is also facilitated by the introduction of a suggestion scheme, whereby any individual member of the staff may make suggestions to improve the working conditions of the organisation.

A suggestion-box system may also be instituted. They will not only yield new ideas but improve the staff morale as well. It is a time-saving system. With such a system of a suggestion box, for every rupee that is spent on programmes soliciting employee suggestions, as per a research study, an average of twenty five rupees worth of practical ideas can possibly be received.

The administrator must listen to his staff attentively so as to derive the essence of their utterances. He may ask such questions that will stimulate them to speak out frankly without any reservation.

It is better for the administrator to listen to good words, however few they may be, for even that much will confer goodness on him.

Kural 416

He, who listens well enough so as to derive the essence thereof will not speak foolishly, even by slip.

Kural 417

No Harsh Dealings

Pretend to be severe in your posture but, let your punishment be milder if you want your long lasting position undisturbed.

Kural 562

It will not be fruitful if an administrator over dominates his staff. That is to say, he should not create a frightful environment in his zone of administration.

A study made in England is reported to have pointed out

the importance of allowing the workers to have spontaneous involvement in their work and the related decisions. In that study, three groups were tested. One was managed in the traditional way of tight control; one allowed the employees freedom to make suggestions, and to choose their own break times; and the third group operated without rules, not soliciting advice of any kind. Tight control is not at all desirable in any administration.

Strict control will normally be followed by severe punishment to the erring individual. Psychologically speaking, severe punishments will lead to adverse effects. When a subordinate is inflicted with a harsh punishment, his career will be affected. He will feel frustrated and lose his self-confidence. Instead of giving him a chance for his self-development, severe punishment will spoil him psychologically. This will not in any way help the administration.

And, there will be side effects upon the other subordinates. When one among them is subjected to deterrent punishment, others will also lose their moral strength to some extent. Even on the usual occasions when they take decisions, they will hesitate to do so and play safe. They will tend to approach the administrator on every occasion seeking directions. Because of such a fear complex, they are likely to err in their decisions which entail severe punishment and they will lose their normal working capacity and initiative. Ultimately, the morale of the organisation will go down.

But, the administrator cannot afford to remain passive like

a mere spectator over the commissions and omissions of his staff, since he is accountable and answerable to his superiors on administration.

Hence what Thiruvalluvar advocates is that the administrator should show to his staff that he always means business, and that he is particular in getting the things done as he plans. He should pose himself to be severe in dealing with any erring staff, with appropriate posture in his look, writing and directions. The very presence of the administrator, or even his image in his absence, should make his people more and more duty-conscious, alert and attentive. But when an occasion arises for the administrator to inflict a punishment upon an erring individual, let him be as mild as possible.

Even such punishment is not to be inflicted merely for the sake of punishing the individual. Any punishment should be carefully worked out and aimed at correcting the erring individual not to repeat the mistake.

Kural 561

His harsh words and highhanded proceedings of punishment will turn out to be like a sharp file that will saw off his otherwise forceful authority in the hierarchy.

Kural 567

Self-assessment

What fault can there be with the king (the administrator) who removes his own faults first, and then cares to scan the faults of others?

Kural 436

The most important aspect of an administrator is his self-assessment and self-management. He himself will be the prime resource he will have to draw upon in responding, and he ought to know ahead of time what he will find there within himself when he needs to look for help. His primary task, therefore, has to be his personal inventory or a self-profile. He should make as impartial appraisal of his personal goals and objectives with respect to his career and circumstances in a given environment. He must measure the strength of his own personal assets, his intellectual ability, resourcefulness, imagination, his grasp of problems that confront him and the interpersonal relationships with those he will have to deal with. His appraisal should also measure the depth and sincerity of his real desire to achieve a given goal—how badly he wants it, what is his personal capacity, mental stamina etc.

Blame not Others

Most of the modern administrators do not do self-appraisal but they count their kudos. For any shortfall or shortcomings, for any prominent mistakes erupting in his administration, the administrator hastens to find fault with someone or other of his subordinates. He fails to be self-critical. But, as a matter of fact, for many of the prominent commissions and omissions, the administrator himself would be the primary cause—by his failure to take timely decisions or sometimes by taking wrong decisions. Instead of appraising and understanding his own mistakes, he resorts to making some of his subordinates the scapegoat. As such, the very way of his administration will prove to be futile. Actually, he ceases to be an administrator and turns into an offender. Hence the first prerequisite for any administrator is to make self-assessment, to do self-appraisal and be self-critical. He must manage himself for the purpose of managing his people.

To be unduly proud, to have undue wrath and to be mean are the three elements that should be absent in an administrator. If the administrator gets rid of these three harmful elements from his thought process and work, he will prosper in his career and his prosperity will be lauded as gracious.

Kural 431

Niggardly dealings, undignified pride and mean pleasure are the blemishes on the part of the head/administrator.

Kural 432

The deadly enemies of an administrator are his own faults. Let him guard against faults as a matter of great concern.

Kural 434

If he fails to guard himself in time from these flaws he will be ruined like the flame-lit straw.

Kural 435

Such and other defects in himself should be recognised for self-appraisal and for self-criticism and the administrator should strive honestly to remove such faults and build spotless personality. Through self-management, he can become an expert in personnel management.

Benevolent Administration

TO START with, it is worthwhile to go through the following propositions as laid down by E N Gladden (*The Essentials of Public Administration*, Staples Press Limited, London 1958).

1) Public administration as the coordinative factor par excellence in the business of the community becomes increasingly important with the growing complexity of civilisation. This does not mean, however, that the complexity of affairs should not be reduced as much as possible by the encouragement of autonomy in social organisation.

2) Public administration is not good in itself as certain modern doctrines tend to imply. It is a means to an end, as it is productive of amenity and welfare contributing to happiness, it soon reaches a point of diminishing returns at which its absence is preferable to its presence.

3) Public administration is concerned not with policy-making but with tactical processes needed for the effective implementation of policy. It is neutral in attitude, professional in conduct and non-political in objective.

4) The absolute aim of public administration is the most economical use of resources to achieve the determined ends.

Its inherent tendencies to expand must be checked by the application of the principle of economy to its own activities.

5) Public administration cannot be effectively conducted through the motive of personal gain and the public administrator must follow a high code of conduct. The public official must live to serve before he serves to live. This means that public administration must rest upon a philosophy of service which induces a high morale among its practitioners. The real success of public administration depends upon the discovery of the means of coupling the normal selfish urges of the individual to the service of a system that avoids the ordinary crudities of private enterprise.

6) Public administration is but one branch of an administration which is widespread in social activity that is also essential to industrial and scientific civilisation.

7) Although the inherent expansion of public administration may be tempered by the impartial professionalism in pursuance of economy, it can only be finally controlled through the understanding of the ordinary citizen.

8) There is a tendency of public administration to get out of balance and to change into bureaucracy, which is one of the diseases of modern society against which all thinking men should strive. Any doctrine, however Utopian in intention, that places bureaucracy on a throne is destined to fail, since public administration, whether distorted into bureaucracy or not, depends upon an external fecundity which itself is constitutionally incapable of inducing motivation and efficiency.

9) For all these reasons the study of public administration,

the perfecting of public service, and the encouragement of the true spirit of civil service in all official are matters of vital concern to all citizens and believers in democracy.

Now look at Thiruvalluvar for his precepts to administrators. He is very much concerned with the individuality of the actionists which is to be duly recognised and appreciated by the administrator.

Individuals can be motivated to perform the organisational tasks effectively if the goals are congruent with their personal goals. They may be led to perceive that they will serve their personal goals by serving in the organisation.

The personal and organisational policies of the administrator will have to include steps for motivating and activating the staff. He must establish an environment in which the employees would feel cared for and be on cordial understanding with their superiors.

Organisational designs should be contingent upon the nature of work and environment. And administrative practices need to suit the background of the work, the people and the culture.

Neither Slackness Nor Forgetfulness

Excellent it is beyond compare
to be ever with wakeful care.

Kural 536

An organisation is analogous to the body of a living being. Every limb of the body is indispensable for functioning of the body in a wholesome manner. The living being cannot afford to be indifferent to any part of its body, however insignificant it may seem to be. Every part has its own significance and a specific role to play. If the body is to have its normal health, every limb of the body has to be intact and in sound health.

Similarly, for betterment of the organisation and for developing and maintaining its morale and productive capacity, every member of the organisation has to be thoughtfully cared for and looked after.

The administrator will have to be fully aware of the need to understand his staff as individuals, to take their personality into account and to regard the entire staff as a team.

Under Staff-Relations there are certain personal matters like individual health, welfare etc., which on the face of it are not primarily the concern of the administration but which, in effect, can have a considerable influence on the results. Personal idiosyncrasies have a perceptible effect upon efficiency and output of the organisation.

Today's management literature indicates that everything in an organisation affects everything else. Hence, human behaviour has to be seen in the perspective of the totality of the situation.

Individuals have their own preferences, their likes and dislikes, their different skills and competences and personal differences. One may like to be left alone to work on a job that requires his own contribution. Another man may like to work with a group and derive great satisfaction in being a member of a group at work.

Disregard of individual differences will cause more problems in the performance of an organisation.

One of the first jobs of the management is to create a system of information and shared objectives that allow everyone to feel involved in the solution of the problems.

As Lord Skiff has put it, 'If people are not treated with respect and if they do not enjoy their work, but regard it as a necessary evil, then there will be conflict'. People will be discontented and organisationally inefficient with productivity, profits and wages generally poor.

The precept of Valluvam for an administrative head to have a thoughtful watch over each and every subordinate was laid down not only for the upkeep of the positive factors of the staff, but also to check and arrest any negative factors like personal motives, vested interests, craving for public property etc, by which the individuals may be swayed.

Forget none in the organisation, watch everybody with wakeful care, miss nothing of the totality—the gain then will be incomparable.

Take Care of the Actionists

Let the king (head/administrator) take care of the good conduct of the actionists as his day-to-day duty, for, if they are not bent, the world would not become crooked.

Kural 520

Before discussing this precept, let us discuss the fast undertaken by Dharam Singh Rawat, an IAS officer in UP, in protest against the bureaucracy and corrupt politicians. This incident was widely reported in *The Indian Express* dated 28th June 1986 and other dailies. He went on fast twice over the same issue—to highlight rampant corruption in the administration. He went on fast for the third time in 14 August 1986.

Responding to the allegation of Rawat, C V Narasimhan who retired as the Director-General of Police in charge of Vigilance and Anti-corruption, says, 'High level bureaucratic corruption cannot exist in isolation. It must have a measure of political support or connivance, or else, it can be put down immediately'. He also asserts that even if the system is corrupt, an honest officer can continue to play his role. 'Of course, there will be pin-pricks, and if you are inconvenient you may be removed from the (particular) post, against which you have relief. But, it can only be a horizontal transfer and you will not suffer financially, a vertical reduction in rank is not possible because of protection under Article 311 of the Constitution.'

A former Finance Secretary (S Guhan) who quit the IAS some years ago says that the time has come when civil servants starting with the higher civil services should come together on a forum, not along trade union lines, but something similar to PUCL to ensure that the rights given to them are protected. They will have to come together and present a concrete charter of demands. There are a larger number of civil servants who are passive victims and not active collaborators in corruption. They can come out to assess their right to function with respect. It is a question of time and this will happen in another five years.

A senior IAS officer, M S Ram, who voluntarily left the

service in 1976, two years prior to retirement finds both the politicians and the civil servants as victims of an 'Indian Tradition of Autocracy'. He says, 'Reading history, I don't find any difference in the attitude of the Maharajas and the politicians of today. And neither the politician, nor the civil servant, feels he is a representative of the people and answerable to them. Humility is lacking in the higher civil services today. The civil servants have become sycophants to the politicians, but lack the element of humility when it comes to the masses'.

When the political administration is obsessed with euphoria of mass popularity and cheap publicity concentrating on vote bank politics, the Actionists at the top political administrative services face dilemmas, as they are subjected to various forms of neglect, threats, transfers, assignment to insignificant positions, etc. and rendered ineffective. To face such a situation they have to recall the status of erstwhile ICS officers who were praiseworthy as steel frames of the administrative body by leaders like Sardar Vallabai Patel. The lead given by people like T N Sehan, T S Krishnamurthy, Romesh C Dutt and N Vittal is worth emulating. Firmness, purity and virtues should be their unwavering guidelines being firm in their actions and strengthening their association, being bold in one voice to say what is right or wrong, putting their feet down and standing firm on their grounds.

Political Bosses vs Civil Servants

Now, the concept of Thiruvalluvar does not differentiate

between career administrators and political administrators as far as the purity of action is concerned. Whether they realise or not, both politicians and civil servants are the representatives of the people, of course the former to a higher degree.

What is true for the civil servants is even more emphatically true for the political administrators. What is complicated for the civil servants is enormously complicated for the politicians who must take into account everybody's interest. The government does not exist for the civil servants. The civil servants exist for the sake of the government and the government exists for the sake of the people.

The politicians are the formal embodiment of the popular desires and aspirations of the people.

It is out of extensive interactions between bureaucrats, political administrators, political leaders and citizens that there are distilled pragmatic thought process, work-ways and the wisdom acceptable to society. Out of the whole comes something that no individual could provide.

It is to the whole we are indebted to if we are well served. And only through all the parts fusing themselves into a whole can we be well served. This is the process of administration in its broadest and most significant meaning.

The hallmark of democracy is the dominance of government by politicians, popularly oriented and chosen as accountable. Politicians, like other folk, range in quality from excellent to able, from good to poor to very poor and terrible. But, their average quality in a well-established democracy is far above the average quality of their respective peoples. The betterment of the government can be achieved by substituting high-grade politicians in place of the inferior ones. And the responsibility of such a replacement rests with the people.

Corruption

As for the corruption or other social evils in public administration or in the society as a whole, neither the bureaucracy nor the political administrators can be held solely responsible. These evils have to be taken as the reflection of the actual condition of the society, or as the indicator of the actual standard of the people at large in any country. We get a government that we deserve.

But it is high time that the administrative heads of various government departments or corporations or heads of political administration took note of the precept of Thiruvalluvar that good conduct or otherwise of the people depends upon the conduct of the actionists. If the actionists are straight, the country will be straight. If they are not taken care of properly in order to enable them to lead their life graciously, it will denote that their hard work has not been properly recognised. As a result, the country will be bound to bend itself.

What is the use of a man's grand saintly postures
if his mind is knowingly bent on evils?

Kural 272

Sincere and hardworking people alone will be particular in obtaining job satisfaction with their sense of dedication to the work. They will not tend to become fraudulent. Only the hypocrites who pretend to be duty-conscious but who are mostly interested in searching for short-cuts to earn wealth will be corrupt. If such people are allowed to flourish freely while the sincere and hardworking people are stranded in humiliating conditions, the character and conduct of the country is sure to go down.

Whoever the actionist may be, he should be taken care of and looked after with due recognition to his sincere actions. He should not be left stranded. Nobody should be allowed to exploit his potential to work. He should be valued and esteemed but not the hypocrites.

This is the most important element of management and administrative philosophy as advocated by Thiruvalluvar for public administration in a welfare state. And this is the only way, as per Valluvam, to set right corrupt life of society. Blaming the political leaders by the bureaucracy or vice versa for the prevailing corrupt practices is not meaningful.

Individual Transformation

Righteousness resides in the hearts of the virtuous
deceit resides in the hearts of the frauds.

Kural 288

Thiruvalluvar does not believe in any missionary movement or in constituting committees for the purpose of eradicating the fraudulent and corrupt practices in public service. He believes only in the individual's transformation. He does not advocate any regimentation of any one section of the population in order to transform the whole lot.

Rabindranath Tagore is also of the same view in this respect. He says:

> I do not put my faith in any new institution, but in the individuals all over the world who think clearly, feel nobly, and act rightly, thus becoming the channels of moral truth. Our moral ideas do not work with chisels and hammers. Like trees, they spread their roots in the soil and branches in the sky, without consulting any architect for their plans.
>
> For all the evils in the present world, the lack of sense of values or the faulty sensing of the values is the main cause. Air is more valuable than anything else for human life. But most of the affluent and aristocratic people choose to live in huge bungalows which lack in the required aeration. They value their so-called prestige of living in such bungalows more than the air (prana) itself!
>
> If people are serious enough in evolving their sense of values in the correct perspective, they will not become mad in running after the futile wealth until their last breath.

The very attitude of one's containing himself in the contentment in life is valued as virtue by Thiruvalluvar. One who is devoid of this attitude will resort to covet the property of others. And such people will be inclined to adopt fraudulent practices. Vices, deceit, hiding, hoarding, etc. will overwhelm their life.

Here are some of the maxims of Thirukkural, throwing the light of wisdom on unsocial elements craving for public property who crop up in public service. These couplets draw attention to the folly of the corrupt folk.

To gather wealth by fraudulent means and to preserve it is just like keeping water in a mud pot of unburned clay.

Kural 660

The gains through fraud may seem to grow limitlessly, but it will perish ultimately.

Kural 283

Far superior is the extreme poverty of the upright than the amassed wealth by fraudulent means by heaping up of sinful deeds.

Kural 657

Desire not the gains through covetousness, for its utility will never be praiseworthy.

Kural 177

Public administration should rest upon a philosophy of service and not on the motive of personal gain. The public officials must live to serve before he serves to live.

Public administration should strive to discover the means of coupling the normal selfish urges of the individuals to the service of a system. The administration must know what motivates individuals and how the individual's goal and the organisation's objectives can be directed to identify with each other.

But, at the same time, every official should understand that he is the representative of the people and that his official as well as his personal life will simultaneously affect the morale of the public.

Management in Thirukkural

Management In General

Perhaps there is no more important area of human activity than managing for all managers at all levels and in all kinds of enterprises who have the basic taste of designing and maintaining an environment in which individuals working together in groups can accomplish presented missions and objectives.

Harold Koontz and Cyril O'Donnel

Essentials of Management, 1978

ALL THE precepts of Thiruvalluvar with regard to different facets of life—conjugal life, domestic life, spiritual life and the life of political administration and career administration—are well founded on a thorough knowledge of human psychology. And the various facets of management and public administration are dealt with in the *Thirukkural* classic with a concrete base of a comprehensive knowledge of human behavior and psychodynamics.

Administrative systems have to be aligned and organised with respect to the prevailing cultural orientation and hence it may differ from country to country. But *Thirukkural* can be considered to have been written at a time when humanity was unstinted with different contradicting factors such as religious faiths, caste, creed etc.

Thiruvalluvar's system of ethics is based on the highest order of excellence. His conception of the good of the community and the duties and responsibilities prescribed for each and every member of the community to contribute to that good is a unique feature of the *Thirukkural.* Thiruvalluvar formulates the most comprehensive and far-reaching philosophy of service to humanity.

Management is the art of administering an organisation, whether it be a business, a non-profit organisation or a government body. Management includes the activities of setting the strategy of an organisation and coordinating the efforts of its employees or volunteers to accomplish its objectives through the application of available resources, such as financial, natural, technological and human resources.

Management includes planning, organising, staffing, directing and controlling an organisation to accomplish the goal or target. It encompasses the deployment and manipulation of human resources, technological resources and natural resources.

Basic Managerial Aspects

IN GENERAL all managers need some basic qualities to man their organisations efficiently and improve the performance. Enthusiasm is one of the basic requirements. First of all, a manager should not be lazy. The next stage will be enthusiasm. Thiruvalluvar chides laziness in a number of couplets.

Four Enemies to be Eschewed

Procrastination, forgetfulness, sloth and sleep
are boats that the self-doomed love to keep.

Kural 605

Four basic qualities which are against progress have been mentioned here so that a good manager carefully avoids them all.

A tendency to lag behind in any field of activity is to be condemned. To forget what is to be done and what is to be maintained spells doom. Idling one's time all along will never give good results. As all these qualities are detrimental to the very existence, it is very essential that a manager takes enough care to shun away from these bad qualities.

Always keep sloth at bay and be busy
to upload prestige of the family.

Kural 602

What is home for a normal human being is organisation for a manager. If a manager wants his organisation as a unique one, he should not give room for sloth at any cost. He should shun it and drive it away with red signals. Only then can he make his organisation ideal.

All these couplets have indicated the necessity to be free from sloth. On the positive side, apart from being free from sloth, a good manager should have initiative and enthusiasm to ensure proper performance.

Possession of zeal alone is everlasting wealth.
Material possessions are fleeting wealth.

Kural 592

'Where there is a will there is a way', is the English proverb. Nothing is difficult for the strong. A strong will can remain with a man and make him successful, though other worldly wealth may depart from him.

Hence, a manager needs enthusiasm in order to achieve his objectives.

Those with enduring zeal won't lament
the loss of wealth possessed.

Kural 593

This couplet corroborates the previous one. When a manager has initiative and strong will, he does not need to bother about temporary setbacks.

Stem length of lily depends on water level.
Men's greatness depends on zeal.

Kural 595

This indicates that the credibility and merit of a manager is indicated by his mental strength. This *Thirukkural* couplet also gives a good example. The height of the lotus reflects the depth of water. Similarly, the rise of a manager to heights in his profession is known by his mental acumen.

If a manager with a strong will takes initiative and works with vigour, fortune will come in search of him and enter his organisation with a boom. 'The world loves only a lover', goes the proverb. Similarly, Dame Fortune loves only a tireless worker and comes to his aid.

Apart from mental strength and initiative, the effort a man puts forth brings him success in his objective.

Effort and Efficiency Indicator

Get not discouraged saying 'It's hard'.
Efforts will bring due regard.

Kural 611

We should not get into a mental fixation. If a job is difficult, a manager should not be afraid of it and shelve it for good. On the other hand, he should explore the possibility of doing it by some other better means. With sustained efforts, he can complete the job and enjoy the happiness from a dream coming true. Satisfaction of carrying through the job is a reward unparalleled.

As the world deserts those who midway shirk,
do not give up your task.

Kural 612

This is a good lesson not only for ordinary human beings but also every manager worth the name. When a manager commences a job, he should put forth his efforts continuously till the objective is achieved. Shirking it midway will only result in waste of time and energy put forth by him thus far. The organisation itself will desert such a manager because he is of no use.

An able minister is one who divides foes' allies,
keeps friends and binds parted ones.

Kural 633

This character of a minister well applies to a manager also. He has to cherish friends so that they may be with him and render all help. He should divide foes so that their energy is not combined and aimed at him. Also, if good and useful people have parted from the organisation, the manager should unite them with the organisation to ensure growth.

Perseverance

This is an oft-quoted *Thirukkural* couplet, advocating sustained efforts. Efforts put forth will definitely ensure success in completion of the job and as a result, prosperity will prevail. On the other hand, if one does not make human effort but is indolent, all the effort made will be lost and the result will be poverty.

Thiruvalluvar has indicated a number of duties and responsibilities and prescribed essential qualities for the ministers. They apply to the managers of the modern world too.

Perseverance leads to prosperity.
Effortlessness results in poverty.

Kural 616

Correct Ourselves

A manager should not be faulted for his action and for this he needs to take necessary precautions. Thiruvalluvar tenders pieces of advice to the king to be free from faults. An ambitious manager can learn a lot from these couplets.

How can a king be blamed if he removes
first his faults, then looks into others.

Kural 436

It is necessary for a manager to ensure that his decisions and actions are free from faults. Then only can he have the moral authority to find fault with others and take corrective measures. His exercise in correcting faults in others will be effective only when he takes care to be faultless himself.

What are the common faults a manager should avoid? Thiruvalluvar has answers to this question as well.

Great indeed is the wealth of those men
who aren't proud, angry and mean.

Kural 431

There are certain faults which are generally found with those in authority. A good manager should take preventive steps to avoid them. Wrath is one such bad quality. The other thing which can wreck a man's future is pride. Next is pettiness or meanness. A manager should take care to avoid these faults altogether for his own sake and for his organisation as well.

Uprightness

Never indulge in self-praise in any mood.
Nor desire deeds bringing no good.

Kural 439

One of the main faults attributed to men in position is boasting. They boast in vain of their power, authority, achievements and so on and so forth. Such boasting is a negative trait which has to be avoided. Also, they should take care that they do not do anything detrimental to the organisation. Because it will only result in wastage of time, money and energy which could have been spent for a better cause. How should one avoid faults? Here also, Thiruvalluvar extends us help.

Prevention is Better than Cure

Even though a fault may seem millet small,
men fearing disgrace deem it palm tall.

Kural 433

One should not consider any fault to be too small and go on repeating them. If a manager wants to avoid disgrace, he should treat even a very minor fault as palm tall and avoid it.

As offence is a foe causing destruction
guard against it with all caution.

Kural 434

Here also, the necessity to be cautious and free from fault is stressed. Just like a treasure keeper guards his treasure, a manager should be watchful that an error does not enter his regime. Because the failure to take cognisance of mistake and avoiding them turns out to be a fatal foe. This indicates that we have to avoid mistakes at any cost.

Seeking the Worthy

Who has fit counsellors and does right deeds
has nothing to fear from foes.

Kural 446

A Manager need not be afraid of frightful competitors if he has worthy friends who know the in and out of the business and advise him on time. This is the gist of this *Thirukkural* couplet.

No enemy can bring any ruin to him
who has friends to rebuke him.

Kural 447

This is a very important lesson in management which we have not so far come across. Our expert friends should guide us in both ways. What is to be done and what is not to be done. If a manager errs, the expert should advise him so that he can take timely action to correct the mistakes before it is too late. To reprieve and reprimand on time is also the duty of the expert advisor.

Guarding against Complacency

What should a good manager avoid? Thiruvalluvar has explained these in a number of couplets. A good performer should never slacken his efforts. He should never forget the job. He should avoid excess in wants (desire) and the job. These negative attitudes spoil the efforts of a good manager.

Forgetting one's duty in excessive happiness
is worse than wrath in excess.

Kural 531

Anything in excess is bad. Everything should be controlled and tuned to the optimum limit. This is a lesson to be learnt by the managers of today. This couplet especially teaches us that joy in excess is more harmful than wrath in excess. Normally, we think joy is good but if it is enjoyed in excess, one forgets one's duties and hence fails in his performance. It is considered worse than wrath in excess. Wrath is counter-productive. If in excess, it may destroy all efforts. On the other hand, just because it is joy, we cannot take it for granted and have it in excess. When in excess it is worse than a negative quality.

As incessant want destroys wisdom,
forgetfulness in duty ruins fame.

Kural 532

Pursue work with unforgetful mind
and nothing hard you will find.

Kural 537

Man proposes, God disposes, says the old proverb. When a strong-willed man proposes, God seconds it, says the new maxim. As such, if a manager commences a job after due analysis and pursues the same vigorously with all the caution and care it deserves, everything can be achieved.

A manager should not be afraid to face problems in whichever manner and shape it comes. He should laughingly encounter them all.

A manager should take care to avoid negligence. Negligence of one's important duties generally comes from overconfidence and indulgence in avoidable rituals. As such, a manager should take care to curtail them and see that necessary and productive details are not curtailed. Negligence spoils performance and reputation. As an example and a byproduct, Thiruvalluvar cites one more aspect, ceaseless wants destroy wisdom. Unnecessary desire applied continuously destroys one's wisdom. As such, a manager has to guard against both. The consequence of negligence as well as desire is expressed emphatically in this couplet.

By way of example, Thiruvalluvar goes on to cite the bad qualities that need to be shunned by a manager, so as to improve his performance.

Overcome Fear and Sloth

As no fortress is fruitful for the fearful,
No fortune is useful for the forgetful.

Kural 534

A king who is fearful of defending or offending will have no fortress. Similarly, a manager who is forgetful cannot achieve anything worth the salt. This couplet makes it clear that a manager should take care to avoid fearfulness as it is a non-starter.

Laugh away the trouble when it comes.
Nothing equals it to conquer pains.

Kural 621

This is a good psychological lesson from Thiruvalluvar. When one frowns at problems, one's mental strength goes down and one will not be able to face them and solve them successfully. On the other hand, if one encounters the problems with a laughing face, one's mind gets the lift it needs. Then, one is able to be in a position to analyse the problem in proper perspective and find a suitable solution. To face troubles with a smiling face is the best way to conquer them. The same idea is reaffirmed by another *Thirukkural* couplet in a different manner.

Who, in grief, do not grieve
make grief itself grieve.

Kural 623

If one is not unduly worried by an incident causing grief, one can make those responsible for the sorrow aggrieved. The mind which handles the situation without any undue worries puts grief itself to grief. This is a good lesson for worrying managers!

Even though misfortune may rise like a flood,
a wise man overcomes it by thoughts bold.

Kural 622

Troubles may come like flood. But if a manager is wise enough to be firm in mind, he can face any amount of trouble with ease and prevent them ab-initio.

Boss as a King

Covet not things which the king cherishes.
This fetches lasting royal riches.

Kural 692

We should leave certain things to the bosses. We should not compete with them. Then only can a manager be favoured by his boss. If his boss finds him as a competitor he may not like him to continue in office, let alone develop.

Know your Safeguards

Guard yourself against grave wrongs.
Or you can't clear king's misgivings.

Kural 693

A manager has to guard himself from all sort of excesses. He should not exceed the power and position delegated to him. However petty or small the excess, he should take necessary precautions to avoid it. It is better to prevent the boss from suspecting his bonafides because once the boss starts suspecting, it is very difficult to clear the suspicion and prove one's worth. Hence, it is better that a manager takes adequate and timely precaution to keep himself away from situations that give rise to doubts.

Do not Misuse your Privileges

Men with vision do no undesirable things
thinking they have the king's blessings.

Kural 699

Just because one is in good books of the boss and he has his grace, one should not indulge in mean activities which undermine the reputation of the boss and one's own. A manager should take enough care to guard against this evil. We might have come across a number of cases in which the closeness to men at the helm of affairs has been misused by those close to them. As such, this is an important lesson to be followed.

Face is the Index of the Mind

A good manager should have some definite personal skills. Reading the minds of others through their facial expression and eyes is one important skill. This has been stressed in a number of *Thirukkural* couplets.

Is there anything more obvious than the face
to tell one's own joy or ire in advance?

Kural 707

Whenever the mind feels, the face expresses. Facial expressions definitely tell what is in the mind. In such cases, what can one do? Here is the solution.

It's enough to stand and look at the face
of those who can read others' thoughts.

Kural 708

A skilled manager puts his skill into action. He stands just before the man and reads what is in his mind from his facial expressions, however subtle it may be.

The true measuring rod of discerning minds
is none but the eye finding all subtleties.

Kural 710

This *Thirukkural* couplet explains the position. What is in one's mind will be well explained through one's eyes. One cannot hide the expression of the eyes. One can learn from the expression of the eyes of another man. Even a microscopic reaction will be expressed in a person's eyes and can be understood by our eyes. A manager aspiring to be successful should develop this talent. Similarly, a manager should be bold enough to express himself properly before his audience.

Express Emphatically

One who binds the learned with lore acquired
is a learned among the learned.

Kural 722

What one has learnt will not serve any purpose unless he is able to express his thoughts and opinions in front of his staff and colleagues. If he is able to express his ideas and impress them, his work is half done. The next couplet is a step ahead.

Impress the scholars with your learned lore.
From greater scholars learn still more.

Kural 724

Apart from impressing one's seniors with one's expressions, a manager has something more to do. He can learn what is required from them. They will only be too glad to permit him to gain from their experiences.

Cultivate Comradery

A manager should know how to develop friendship with deserving people. Here also Thiruvalluvar is able to guide us with a number of couplets.

True friendship is not for mere enjoyment
but to reprove faults of one's mate.

Kural 784

A friend is often quite useful. He will not stop laughing, enjoying and having fun. Whenever we commit a mistake knowingly or unknowingly, he will point it out and try to correct us. Thus, a true friend is really useful.

Amity rescues from ruin, shows good paths
and shares pains in times of crisis.

Kural 787

The help rendered by a true friend is outlined in this *Thirukkural* couplet. He saves us from ruin by showing us where we err and teaching us how to correct it. Also, when we are sad due to various reasons, he shares the pain with us.

He also shows us the right path, so that we may not err again and come to grief but succeed.
The next couplet explains how a true friend acts.

Friendship hastens to save friends in distress
like hands quickly restoring slipping dress.

Kural 788

This is a very fine example. When one's dress slips from the waist, the hand immediately rushes to hold it. Similarly, a true friend rushes to help when one is in grief so that one is less sad. After this knowledge from Thiruvalluvar, no manager will hesitate to cultivate true friendship. If friendship is going to yield so much of good, then one has to be careful in losing friends. Thiruvalluvar is able to guide us even on this score.

One's nature, lineage, flaws and relations:
know them and make friends.

Kural 793

Before choosing friends, you have to take all these aspects into consideration. The character of the persons is of utmost importance. Next comes his family background. If he is a good man and has a good family background, it is worth having him as your friend. Then his defects or lapses should also be taken into consideration, lest we lament later. If they are of minor nature, we can ignore them. Or else, they will be deciding factors in discarding one's friendship. The quality and number of kin of your proposed friend is also a major factor in choosing friends. A good manager must weigh all these aspects before choosing good and worthy friends. The process of choosing friends is elaborated further by Thiruvalluvar.

Seek men who make you feel, reprove errors
and teach you the right ways.

Kural 795

As we already saw in a previous couplet, it is not to laugh and enjoy alone that we cultivate friendship. A true friend will help you when you do wrong. He will point out your lapses and chide when you commit mistakes and show you the right path even at your displeasure. The final advice of Thiruvalluvar is this:

Seek only the friendship of the blameless.
Give something and give up the base.

Kural 800

One should make friends with those with an unblemished record. At the same time, the friendship of mean people who are not worthy should be discarded at any cost. Even though we might have to pay for severing the friendship it should be done so that it does not ruin your career.

Even if friends do deeds unasked out of liberty,
the wise would approve it lovingly.

Kural 804

Real friends will help you and do things on your behalf and for your sake, even though you have not asked for their help. You should be able to understand the assistance and accept it in the right spirit.

A close friend won't listen to rumours vile.
Even when hurt, he hails the day well.

Kural 808

Good and cherished friends tolerate even wrongs done to them by their good old friends. They don't lament over minor irritants. While cherishing worthy friendship, one should be careful enough to discard bad and false friendship.

Fear cheats who smile sweeter in front
but are full of guile in their heart.

Kural 824

Some foes will pretend to be your friends. Their faces will be adorned with harmless smiles whereas their hearts will be full of cunning ideas to bring you down. You should identify those people and discard their friendship.

Folded hands of foes may conceal arms.
Even their tears may hide evils.

Kural 828

This is an oft-quoted *Thirukkural* couplet which shows, to what extent foes can deceive. Even though one may appear to pay respects with folded hands, he may be hiding arms in his folded hands to kill you.

The same thing had happened in the case of Mahatma Gandhi. Godse came to Gandhi with folded hands and said 'Namaste Bapuji'. Immediately, he took out a gun and shot the Mahatma dead. What Thiruvalluvar had said two thousand years ago came true in this century. As such, a manager should be careful of his foes disguised as friends.

Feign laugh and love but break amity
with those who extol but have enmity.

Kural 829

Some enemies will outwardly show friendship towards you. At the same time, in their heart of hearts, they may nurture ill will towards you. With such people, you should also act friendly towards them but at the same time, you should find ways and means to discard their friendship.

Another point Thiruvalluvar stresses is folly. Even educated people can be governed by folly unless they are careful. Let us look at what Thiruvalluvar writes about this.

Folly foretells Fall

Fool of fools is the one who always learns,
realises, teaches but never practices.

Kural 834

Even though a manager is educated and he can teach others about several things, he might not be capable of controlling his own foolish acts. If so, he is the most foolish of all the fools on earth. Thiruvalluvar chides such educated people who cannot control folly in unequivocal terms. What is folly? Here also Thiruvalluvar is able to guide us through a number of couplets.

Folly is clinging to what is harmful
and leaving what is fruitful.

Kural 831

When we stand to gain while choosing one path and stand to lose by choosing the other, if we choose the latter path it is definitely an obvious folly. A good manager should first of all avoid such glaringly foolish acts. What are the other dimensions of folly which one should avoid? Thiruvalluvar is very clear on this score too.

Lack of shame, desire, love and regard
are the marks of the stupid.

Kural 833

One should feel ashamed to do things below one's dignity and decorum. One should have aim in all one's endeavours. One should not show gross indifference to one's duty. One should take care to maintain anything worth the name by listing to samc. If a man desists from all these good qualities, it is sheer folly. Stupidity and vanity is also chided by Thiruvalluvar.

What is utter folly is sin of pride
that boasts 'I am learned'.

Kural 844

If an unwise man thinks himself wise and declares to others to that effect, then vanity or stupidity is at its worst form. As such, one should not have any pretence whatsoever regarding what one knows and what one does not know.

Pretence of learning what one hasn't learnt
puts to doubt what one has really learnt.

Kural 845

It is very important to remember what is explained through this couplet. If one pretends as if one knows things which one does not know, others will even doubt what one really knows.

A fool who knows not and heeds not the wise
is a plague until he dies.

Kural 848

What sort of a fate is predicted by Thiruvalluvar for such stupid people? One who does not know by himself, nor will listen to others for knowledge, is supposed to be affected by some serious disease. Therefore, pretence and vanity are stupidity which will spell ruin and hence a good manager should avoid them at any cost. Another negative factor a manager should avoid is hatred, which spells disaster.

Hatred breeds Discord

Hatred is a disease that breeds
discord among all beings.

Kural 851

This negative quality does not affect you and the one you hate. But it spreads ill will among all those connected with both sides.

A perverted genius longing for hostility
will not see the truth causing victory.

Kural 857

Once you start hating somebody or nurture hatred towards some section, then your mind is completely biased and prejudiced. Under the circumstances, you cannot see the truth because the maya (illusion) of prejudice created by hatred hides the truth from your vision. As such, in order to see the truth you should eschew hatred. This is a good lesson to one, and more pertinent to managers in particular.

All sufferings spring only from animosity.
Wealth of virtues flows from amity.

Kural 860

When we want goodness, naturally we have to choose the path of amity. Even though one should not nurture hatred and enmity on his own, he should be careful enough to identify the enemies within and outside and keep them at bay. Otherwise, managing will become difficult.

The world abides by the greatness of rulers
who turn their foes into allies.

Kural 874

It is better if a man is capable of making friends out of foes. Such a man spells good omen for the whole world. But it may not be possible always. Some people would not like to be friends. They would like to remain foes. One should be careful of such people.

If one knows ways, fortifies and himself protects,
vanity of foes will surely collapse.

Kural 878

For dealing with those who would like to remain enemies out of pride, you should know how to defend yourself so that the prides of enemies fall. A manager should also be careful about the enemies within.

Unrepenting hidden enmity breeds evils
and keeps away one's relatives.

Kural 884

When the foe within is capable of fomenting trouble and spoiling relationship with kinsmen, it should be our duty to eliminate him. We should not neglect the foe, underestimating him.

While taking enough precaution to eliminate enmity from within and outside, one should take necessary care that he does not offend great people.

Humbleness

One who does great things, if he is really a great man, is very humble and modest. He never boasts about things he has achieved. The same idea is stressed in different words in another couplet.

Greatness is free from vanity.
Pettiness rides on vanity.

Kural 979

The major dimension of greatness is to be free from insolence. Otherwise, one will be considered as petty. To be great and to achieve great things one should have necessary courage.

Glory is doing with mental fervour.
Disgrace is a life sans ardour.

Kural 971

This couplet lays stress on the quality of courage which makes a man do great things and live in limelight.

Another character Thiruvalluvar suggests is the noble quality of being sublime.

Doing Good

Of what avail is the perfection of character
if it fails to do good even to an evil-doer?

Kural 987

A man's nobility should be so sublime that he should do only good even to those who cause grief to him. This is indeed the highest form of sublimity expected of an individual.

All good deeds are indeed natural to the great
who are duty-conscious and perfect.

Kural 981

Those who are sublime in nature consider it as their duty to be good and to do good things.

Goodness of heart is the virtue of the great.
All else are not at all great.

Kural 982

Great people who are sublime in nature consider good character as the most valuable thing they can possess. Due to their experience they know that it is character which enhances one's prestige and makes one great.

Courteous Mannerism

All these teachings a manager must remember and practise, so as to have a good image in the society in which he works and lives. Courtesy is another good quality, advocated by Thiruvalluvar.

One can gain virtue called courtesy
if one is accessible easily.

Kural 991

If a man holding a high post is polite and easily accessible to people, courteousness comes to him automatically. Being polite and accessible are two dimensions of courtesy, as pointed out in this couplet.

Benign Attitude

All the world will commend the excellence
of men who serve all with justice and grace.

Kural 994

This couplet stresses that the world will applaud courteous people. Being courteous is not only a virtue but it also pays. Other two dimensions of courtesy are also explained in this couplet. They are being just and benign. A courteous manager stands to gain on all counts. Another quality one should nurture is sensitivity to shame, says Thiruvalluvar. Thiruvalluvar also talks highly of promoting family welfare. But as far as we are concerned, we can equate this with an organisation's welfare.

Nothing is indeed more dignified than saying,
I'll dutifully raise my family's well-being.

Kural 1021

A man who wants to work for the uplift of his organisation should take a vow to work for it without any slackness whatsoever. Such a vow and follow-up is definitely the greatest thing one can do.

One's lineage grows by one's ceaseless acts
based on effort and profound genius.

Kural 1022

Two main things a manager should have in order to keep up his organisation have been mentioned here. One is wisdom. Mere static wisdom alone will not do. What the wisdom dictates he should carry out through his efforts in order to ensure the uplift of the organisation.

Ripe Wisdom and Devotion to Duty

God fastens His robes and rushes to help him
who strives to exalt his home.

Kural 1023

When one decides to work hard for the sake of his organisation, even Almighty God will come to one's help and guide him the proper way. Why cannot we work hard for the prosperity of our house when God himself is prepared to help? Thiruvalluvar also blesses those who work for their race.

Who strains ceaselessly to elevate his family
gains success spontaneously.

Kural 1024

If one is prepared to work hard for one's house, one need not be unduly worried about the end. The end will be only to his gain.

If one wants to have better human relations, the first thing one should possess is communication skills. Communication skills can be developed by proper understanding and training. This subject is being dealt with in the chapter titled, Communication Skills.

Organisational Relations

ORGANISATION IS made up of people. It is the human element involved in achieving the objectives of the management. Hence a structure with different limbs, with different people with effectiveness, exists. One thread linking the structure is the personal relationship. This personal relationship can make the 'personnel', 'personal' contributors towards the goal.

Hence the organisational relations is very vast and very wide and relates to human relations, leadership qualities, domestic relations, social relations and public relations. These subjects are dealt in detail as the subdivisions of this subject.

Leadership

'Without leadership, resources of production remain as resources and never become production. Leading has three components—motivation, leadership and communication. Leadership must be based on an understanding of what motivates people, and hence a good knowledge makes people comfortable and this is vital for a leader. Leadership involves selection of an approach depending upon the situation and an ability to inspire people to follow. Communication is the means by which leadership is finally accomplished and it is really a question of what to communicate, to whom, how and when. Ultimately, the effectiveness of an organisation will depend upon the extent to which leaders are able to discharge their functions'.

Have a Purpose

Men of greatness do rare deeds
in proper and perfect ways.

Kural 975

If we could pick one thing we most wanted out of our job and our life, what would it be?

While many of us chase money, prestige and recognition, the single most important thing you can achieve is meaning. Having a purpose in everything you do makes every day valuable and every outcome, good or bad, worthwhile.

Barbara Miller is a consultant who studies the workplace and the quality of workers lives for high-tech companies. Barbara explains, the global market-place is requiring organisations to be open around the clock now, and that is changing both work and lives of high-tech employees.

Barbara warns companies that they cannot overlook the strain they place on families, when the workday expands or becomes limitless. She reports that many companies talk about work-life balance but then don't practice it. Just putting in work-life programmes isn't going to help people have work-life harmony. We've really got to take a look at the way organisations are structured and change our work places accordingly.

Barbara found one organisation in which all its engineers were on call every weekend in case of a client emergency. Anyone could be called away from their families at any time. They never really relaxed because they didn't know if they were really off or not. Attrition rate was very high because many of these people questioned why they needed a job that prevented them from having a family life.

Ultimately, Barbara's recommendations were followed, and a new policy was set in. In the new schedule, weekend shifts were staffed voluntarily by workers who received week days off in return.

Feeling there is meaning in your life is eight times more likely to produce satisfaction than a high income.

Winners are Made, Not Born

Tho' human beings in their birth are the same
by avocations their worth isn't alike.

Kural 972

People succeed and reach where they are following strategic plans. They learn what it takes to get ahead.

We understand that to build a house, it takes a plan, a blueprint, but we sometimes forget that to build a successful life also it takes an honest and flexible blueprint.

Chef Walter Potenza owns three thriving Italian restaurants in Rhode Island. He studied and trained to be a chef, but he sees now that his abilities are the product of a lifetime of education. When he opened his first restaurant, 'All of a sudden my schooling, the knowledge and the history of my family, the respect and ethics of my father came into play. It made me an academic, a person who explored the food business'.

And the learning never stops. 'One of the secrets is, it's a business where you constantly need to stay on top. Chefs are not born.' Walter explains that the process continues for him. Every day: 'I'm an obsessive reader. Every time you read a book, you get ideas. Then you introduce your ideas into your workplace. You make more work for yourself, but you make that work better.'

And success in the cooking business is something he has a clear definition of: 'The success that I would like to have is to be remembered as a man who was innovative, who believed in authenticity and the culture of Italian cuisine in America. Food is the link to the past and to the heart. Success to me is not how much money you make. But if at the end of the day I was able to make fifteen out of twenty customers happy, I'm a happy man.'

A case study research on business executives reveals that 98 per cent see their position as the result of plans and strategy and that more than half credit their use of a successful person as an example, to help define that plan.

Experience is a Continuous Process

Dig deeper the sand-well, more water flows.
Read deeper, more wisdom grows.

Kural 396

Take the first chance you have to get into the field of your dreams.

Even if the job itself is not what you want, you will get a better idea of what that line of work entails, and you will begin to prepare yourself for the job you ultimately desire. Or you might find out, it's not the right job for you and that your future plans need to be adjusted.

Fred Marzocchi grew up with dreams of drawing for a living. 'There are many ways to make a living with your sketch book, but advertising was one of them.'

When he couldn't find a job as a commercial artist, Fred became desperate for experience. He found a large drug store chain with an in-house advertising unit and offered to work for literally nothing. They took him up on the offer, and within weeks not only had he gained professional experience, but the drug store decided to pay him for his efforts.

After working for a number of advertising agencies, Fred went on to open his own graphics design and photography business. He often looks back on the offer to work without pay. 'I just needed a chance, a start in this business, and I haven't had to work for free since', he says with a smile.

Explore Opportunities

College students who serve in internships are 15 per cent more likely to find employment after graduation and 70 per cent believe they are better prepared for the workplace because of their internship experience.

The secret of corporate success lies in continuously exploring opportunities and in exploiting them systematically. While the former is an ongoing process, the latter requires swift actions at appropriate times. There has to be a clear demarcation of approach between what is to be done before the zero hour and how it is to be done at the stroke of zero hour. When one waits for the zero hour he should be cautious about not giving any signals regarding his moves. Then when the time comes he should strike the death blow, swift and strong.

Early Experiences

People absorb a tremendous amount of information and learn significant lessons from their earlier experiences. We begin our careers as almost empty notebooks, and as we progress, our mind fills with notations and observations. The first few pages of our mental notebooks are filled with our first experiences.

The potential for difficulty arises, as we try to apply those early lessons to situations in which they are not relevant. Take note of experiences, but realise there are situations where your experiences are no longer applicable.

Schwann Bicycle was the leader in the industry for a hundred years. Edward Schwann, the fourth generation of Schwann's in the business, took control in 1979. Thirteen years later, the bicycle company was on life support, having watched its market share fall by 60 per cent.

Analysts attributed the decline of the company to a refusal to live in the present. Because it was family-owned, Edward Schwann refused outside financing when the company began to show signs of weakness. Because Schwann was the name in bicycles, Edward Schwann refused to spend money on keeping the brand name in consumer's consciousness. Because Schwann was always the kind of company that operated on a handshake and long-term commitment, Edward Schwann agreed to outsource all their manufacturing to the same Chinese supplier, Giant Manufacturing, without adequately protecting Schwann's long-term interests.

By the end, in 1992, Schwann Bicycle was seventy-five million dollars in debt and losing a million per month. No investor would come near the company until it could be picked up for next to nothing in a bankruptcy sale. Product recognition among children dropped to close to zero. And Giant Manufacturing ended its deal with Schwann.

The company declared bankruptcy, and the Schwann family lost all control over the family's business. Edward Schwann's explanation for the fall? 'We are where we are.' To which one family member responded, 'Where we are is out of business because you were asleep at the wheel'.

Who adapts not, knows not his limitation.
And boasts will be damned to perdition

kural 474

He who does not adapt but praises himself without knowing his limitation will quickly perish.

Beginning is Not an End in Itself

It is known that 95 per cent display a particular commitment to sectors in which they experience their first success.

Ultimately, this tendency leads to missing opportunities in other segments of the market and unrealistic enthusiasm for their chosen sector.

Learn well whatever is worthy of learning.
Then act according to that learning.

Kural 391

What is the great common denominator of intellectual accomplishment? In maths, science, economics, history or any other subject, the answer is the same, great thinkers notice patterns.

They see patterns no one else has thought of, patterns no one else has paid any attention to. Thinkers notice what goes along with what, and they consider the meaning behind those patterns.

Take time to consider patterns in your world that you've never thought about before.

I don't care what you do; you have to understand how things work. 'Not just thinking about what you're doing, but about what you're not doing', says George Bedrock.

'Now my business is waste. It's not glamorous, but it's important. But what we're not doing enough of it is finding natural techniques to reduce waste.'

That's why George, of California's Ecology Farms, a commercial waste management company, researches 'vermin-stabilisation'. That's the process of using worms to transform waste into a useful product. Bedrock supervises the use of 160 million worms that eat their weight in yard waste every day and convert the waste into soil nutrient.

It's the only real solution to the green waste problem. People are not going to give up growing lawns, gardens and golf courses. We can take what they throw out and recycle it 100 per cent.

Bedrock calls the worms' endless appetite for waste 'the equivalent to a perpetual motion machine'. He says we can build super-computers that can do a billion calculations a second, but when it comes to breaking down green wastes, there's no computer to do the job. But we have to do it, and we have to keep looking for better ways. And when you do it right, you not only help the earth, you'll become rich in the bargain.

Academic achievement, regardless of the subject matter, is characterised by an ability to decipher complex ideas and relationships. Experiments in language, maths, and science show that the most basic building block of learning is independently observing patterns.

Learn to gain Knowledge and Wisdom

Who learn like the poor before the rich
are great; the rest are low very much.

Kural 395

Let us try to teach someone who doesn't work with computers, how much a computer might make their job easier. The most common reaction we find is stark reluctance. Why would anyone be against learning something that might make their job easier? Often, it is because they fear that something that makes their job easier might one day take over their job.

Teaching is like asking someone to go on a trip. Just as no one is going to take us up on an invitation to travel on a trip from which they would never return, people will be reluctant to participate in learning about their own obsolescence.

When we try to teach anyone something new, we have to make it clear from the outset that the destination is someplace we'd all like to go.

What do I need that for? Jack protested when his grand-daughter asked why he didn't use a computer. Jack had been a farmer all his life and had gotten along fine for fifty years without a computer.

His grand-daughter gave him twenty examples of things he could do with a computer, such as keep track of his expenses or plan his growing schedule, and each time Jack replied that he has been doing those things without a computer.

'What about the weather? What about reports we could get in an instant?'

Finally Jack relented, and a seventy-year-old farmer who had never set his hand on VCR was using a computer to track every aspect of his farm. Jack admitted old habits die hard. 'I get stubborn, like anybody else. I don't need every new-fangled thing to do this job, but every now and then a piece of equipment does help.' Feelings of self-threat is the single biggest obstacle in gaining knowledge.

Firmness of Action

With whatever hardships you are beset,
boldly do deeds that bring delight.

Kural 669

Perspective is a powerful force. From a young age we are taught to hold certain expectations, and those expectations influence how we see the world.

Stereotypes inculcated in us when we were children may be affecting how we evaluate other people and even how we evaluate ourselves.

Nobody chooses rationally to limit their aspirations, deny themselves opportunities, and misjudge other people's talents based on a set of stereotypes. But that is just what we do without even thinking about it because stereotypes alter our view of the world.

In rural northern New Hampshire, the Women's Rural Entrepreneurial Network (WREN) is helping hundreds of women make an income from their homes. WREN'S members run the gamut from women selling handmade crafts in their spare time to women offering professional services such as graphic arts design and book binding full-time.

WREN'S director, Natalie Woodruff, says the group helps bring together women who otherwise might be isolated and feel there are no opportunities available to them. The members feel empowered to succeed and are more likely to overcome the scepticism that rural women working from home face when they try to make a living. These women get more than their share of discouragement from people who act like they are seven-year-olds selling lemonade in their front yard.

WREN connects these work-at-home women with a network of women of all ages and professions. There are attorneys and traditional business managers or owners who donate their time to WREN, and these two very different women can greet each other on the street and feel a bond. WREN crosses all those barriers—economic, cultural, and educational—so that women can see their capabilities and their connections with each others.

Women who are creating and supporting themselves should feel good about what they do.

Great Time, Greater Action - Foresight

The wise who foresee pain of crisis
guard against surprise shocks.

Kural 429

This couplet deals with the foresight expected of a good manager. A good manager should not only get along well with the present but also think about the future and plan well.

For planning well ahead of time, he should anticipate all the handicaps and opposition he may come across while executing the various programmes in order to implement the policies of his company. After he anticipates the handicaps, he should have a plan of action to counter them and carry out his programme successfully. 'To be forewarned is to be fire armed.' As suggested by Thiruvalluvar, a manager who anticipates evil will not be surprised by the handicaps which he may come across in future.

Better do deeds whenever feasible, or else
act after finding proper time and place.

Kural 673

There are occasions, though infrequent, in corporate history and the executive's time frame, when the going is too good. It is at this time that an executive should do all that he had planned to, and also other things which he thought were otherwise difficult and impossible. A good executive will ensure that he not only catches the bus, but also extracts the benefit of whatever the traffic can bear.

Judge the mode of completion, hurdles and gain
before you plunge into an action.

Kural 676

The whole world is his who acts
at the right time and place.

Kural 484

Age Doesn't Matter

Whatever our dreams are, we practically hear a clock ticking. Our family, our friends, even the media all make us wonder when we are finally going to be 'there' and why we aren't there yet.

But there are no age restrictions on success. It takes as long as it takes, and when you reach it, you won't reject success because you're not of the right age for it.

'There are people on top, and then there are people who don't matter. That's how I felt', admits Nathan, who works in advertising in New York. 'I looked down on myself for not being where I wanted to be, and I suffered through every day, like it was my personal humiliation.'

'I didn't take pride in what I did. I practically created a fictional job description for myself, whenever anybody asked me what I really did.'

Nathan says that in his business, 'There's nothing but perception. We don't make better mouse traps, we don't make anything, we sell perception, and our jobs are perceptions. It was like I heard this clock ticking, with each day bringing me closer to failure'.

Nathan sought help from a career coach who asked him who he was really competing with and why. 'When I said, I guess I was competing with everybody in the company because I wanted to be on top. She said, "Well, if you were on top of the company, then you'd be competing with every other company to be bigger than them". Basically, she made me see that there was no way to win this contest and that I could either sit back and enjoy the ride or keep trying to race to a place I could never get to.'

Nathan's perspective shifted. 'Now I try to keep my focus on doing the best work I can, and I know that I'll get where I'm going to when I'll get there.'

Age is unrelated to people's commitment to their job and their level of job performance.

So manage your time and your timing too!

A good manager should be a good leader. Napoleon used to say, 'There are no bad soldiers. There are only bad captains'. The end result depends on the leadership capacity of a manager. If he leads his team properly, he is a good manager, not a performer.

What are the leadership qualities expected of a good manager? Let us turn to Thirukkural for advice.

Unfailing Courage, Charity, Wisdom and Zeal

Unfailing courage, charity, wisdom and zeal.
These four are qualities regal.

Kural 382

In this couplet, Thiruvalluvar has advocated four leadership qualities. Just like a king leads his country, a manager leads his department or company.

1) Hence, the manager should face all the problems encountered by him in the pursuit of his department or company's objectives, with courage. There is no way of hiding oneself from problems.

Suppression is not a solution and unless taken by the horns, one day the problems will grow bigger rather than diminish. Hence, in order to solve them, it is necessary to face them with courage. Moreover, only when a leader shows courage others will follow suit.

2) The next quality pointed out by Thiruvalluvar to become a successful leader is 'award giving'.

In ancient times, kings used to be bountiful in disbursing awards and gifts. In case of modern management, the award procedure (incentive) may be somewhat different. It should be based on a pragmatic pattern. Award procedure helps in motivating workers because positive reinforcement is the best method for motivation. As such, the award procedure for motivating people in different fields to achieve the desired objectives should be properly streamlined. If it is done, it will be a very good tool in the hands of a manager in achieving his objectives effectively.

3) The third quality mentioned here is knowledge. If a manager has to successfully manage his department, he should have thorough knowledge of the chosen field. Knowledge is necessary in order to understand the functioning of the department and to find solutions to the various problems encountered. Only with proper knowledge will he be in a position to issue proper instructions to his subordinates and clear their doubts and guide them. In order to gain the respect of coworkers and to have fruitful discussions with his colleagues and senior officers, knowledge in the chosen field is a must for a modern manager.

4) The next quality, which is expected of an effective manager, is zeal. Zeal is something which spurs a man into action, without zeal one cannot take any initiative. A manager who has no zeal will be happy to maintain his routine and avoid experiment with novel or revolutionary methods of accomplishing goals. Hence, in order to take initiative and to venture into new activities and face up to new challenges, a manager needs zeal. Also the level of zeal or enthusiasm shown by a manager inspires his whole team and spurs others into action in a chain reaction.

Love, modesty, charity, mercy and truthfulness
are five supporting pillars of perfectness.

Kural 983

In the first instance we discussed four good qualities of a leader. This deals with five more qualities, which make a good manager a leader.

Continuing with the concept of the traits of a leader, five qualities are mentioned. He should be a person who is conscious of the policies of the King (Corporate mission) and who implements them by virtue of his knowledge and communication skills. Of course, he will also be one who initiates suitable action at the appropriate time. May be there are thousands of unsung Chanakyas even in corporate kingdoms.

Firmness, nobility, concern, lore and efforts:
an ideal minister has these five traits.

Kural 632

Average people are everywhere around you. They entice you into being more like them, by offering their acceptance and by leading you to believe that everyone else is already more like them than like you.

But the 'average person' sales pitch leaves out that you will be sacrificing your goals, individuality, and unique ideas and that you will lead a life determined more by the preferences of the group than by you.

'A person who wants to be a leader must turn his back to the crowd', says the sign on Ty Underwood's desk. Ty runs a job placement service that works with laid-off and chronically underemployed workers.

'When I got here, there was an attitude that this was all a show to keep the agency's funding. We'd show up, have the clients come in to fill out some papers, then send them on their way. Nobody was behaving as if there was important work to be done; nobody was behaving as if there was potential to be tapped here.'

His first task was to change everything. To two-thirds of the staff, he minced no words: 'Here's your resignation. Sign it.' Now, each day begins with the promise that, 'Everyone who walks through this door can do more. That goes for the counsellors and the clients.'

Two years later, Ty took over an office he considered an embarrassment and turned it into a model, with a job placement record of 71 per cent.

Psychologists have observed that bad habits can spread through an office like a contagious disease. Employees tend to mirror the bad behaviours of their co-workers. Corporate history of India has many examples of native intelligence establishing and expanding business empires. It is a pity that modern management studies have undermined the importance of basic common sense.

Whether he is a leader or a manager, for that he has to be a human being first. Hence, the more humane he is, the more successful he shall be. Love shown by him will be repaid in abundance. Hence, he will be able to lead his team successfully. Truth in his speech and action will keep him in good stead and add respect to his leadership and his team members will follow suit. Hence, it will become easy for him to achieve his objectives. Regard shown to elders and seniors also help in all important activities since their help and guidance is available to him whenever and wherever required.

One more important duty of the executive is to place facts to the deciding authority, whether the latter knows them or not, likes them or not, wants them or not. Thus it is an inescapable responsibility to firmly persuade the authorities, though they may be unwilling to listen. There can be a tendency with the executives sometimes, to unwillingly 'let die' after making a token protest. It is but natural that the executive is closer to the ground and hence knows the facts and figures and so the consequences. On the other hand, the boss or the authority, like a king, is far from ground realities. It is the executive who has to be the nursing link. He should not be tired of the indifference of the authorities, but should have the perseverance to make the boss see the light.

Sanguine Self-interest

Who seek the truth breaking bonds
will be free from worldly ills.

Kural 359

What is the difference between people who willingly take work home with them on the weekends and people who scoff at the idea?

What is the difference between people who work hard all day and people who do as little work as they can possibly get away with?

What is the difference between people who sign up for night school and those who can't imagine going back to school?

What is the difference between the most driven and the laziest person? Self-interest.

Most of us do what we do because of self-interest; we think it's the best thing for us. Those who work hard do so because they believe there is a reward awaiting them that not only justifies their efforts but also demands their dedication. Those who do not expend themselves do so because they cannot see the long-term benefit of work outweighing the short-term benefit of laziness.

Gwen got her start training dogs and soon realised she was really training their owners. 'I would teach people about reacting consistently to what the dogs did, so that good behaviour was rewarded and bad behaviour punished. And I thought to myself, it's not the dogs that are being inconsistent here, it's the people.'

Gwen sees all kinds: 'You have the gigglers who say, "Isn't that cute", when the puppy grabs their socks out of their hands and then get upset when the puppy goes for the socks, the shoes, the couch.' You have couples where one takes the strict approach and the other is in cahoots with the dog, covering up when the dog does something wrong.

'What dogs want', says Gwen, 'is your love, attention, and treats. If you make it perfectly clear and consistent, what it will take to get that reaction, your dog will behave because of self-interest', Gwen believes. 'If you are too lazy to be consistent with your dog, or if you really don't care what happens to your socks and shoes, then your lack of interest will come across.' Self-interest and rewards are the most significant factors in predicting dedication and satisfaction towards work. It accounts for about 75 per cent of personal motivation toward accomplishment.

The present-day approach to the qualities of a manager is that he is an important instrument in achieving organisational objectives and hence falls into the slot of Staffing under 'Organising' which is the second broad step in the theory of management. So we have a fragmentation of the executive profile covering a production versus people-oriented approach or a leadership theory or the Johari Window (a technique used to help people better understand their relationship with themselves and others). These approaches to the attributes of a manager lack the broader perspective of a true executive, though, there are many management books which talk about the qualities of an executive.

There is a prescription of five essential qualities, viz. the tenacity of purpose, good background, concern for the welfare of the people, profound learning and perseverance. May be this does not sound like the usual mathematical model (which perhaps reduces human beings to a pair of numbers on the X and Y axes) or algebraic version (X and Y theory) of the executive. An executive is seen as a person with a passion for people as well as production.

Another quality of a good leader is explained in the Thirukkural couplet below.

Criticism – Ladder to Creativity

The world lives under the sway of ruler
who endures words bitter to the ear.

Kural 389

A good leader or for that matter, a good manager, should never be afraid of criticism. He should tolerate criticism raised against him because only if he is tolerant, his faults will be pointed out to him so that he can take necessary remedial action to correct them in time.

If he does not tolerate bitter words, then only flattery will reach his ears. He will know what has happened only when the whole project has failed or the whole empire has collapsed. Then it will be too late for him to take remedial action. But if he is tolerant, his faults will be pointed out to him, in which case neither will he be able to brush aside nor absorb all criticism raised against him. This will lead to corrective measures which will save the company. Here also Thiruvalluvar is able to guide the modern manager.

Whatsoever is heard, from whomsoever
to discern the truth is wisdom clear.

Kural 423

Someone may criticise you while someone else may praise you. One may be a great scholar or may be an illiterate. A learned person may use high-sounding words, technical jargon, while an illiterate may use the native language. Also, the appearance of each man or position held by each man in society may be different.

A good leader will not differentiate among people. But he will listen to them and analyse their statements point by point in order to understand the underlying ideas and bring out the truth which is relevant to him and make use of it.

Because it is not the man or his appearance but the underlying ideas that count.

Holding back before the wise
is the best of all virtues.

Kural 715

We have a lot to say and only a short time in which to say it. The natural tendency is to try to pack in as much as we can.

Think before you Leap

To shun what is useless and what is ruinous, besides temptation, is real courage and it is a quality of a good manager. Let us go to the next couplet.

Think first and then venture on an act.
To venture and then think is a fault.

Kural 467

This is a very good suggestion for all practising managers. Be it a new policy, a new idea, a new scheme, a new product or a new process, whatever the manager takes up for implementation should be accepted only after he has given a lot of thought to it and about the pros and cons of all the elements involved. Only then should he take a decision.

If a manager takes up a scheme for execution and thinks about it later, it will be ruinous and against the interest of the company or the department he leads. It may result in the loss of money, manpower and time, and last but not the least 'image'. Let us look at the popular English proverb: 'Think before you leap'.

Hence, before venturing into anything new a manager has to think thoroughly and only then come to a conclusion.

The wise discern what is in store.
But fools lack in that lore.

Kural 427

In a previous couplet, we saw that a good leader can foresee the handicaps to his programmes in advance and take necessary remedial measures. In this couplet also, the same idea is reiterated but in a different manner.

A wise leader foresees what is to come whether it is good or bad. Only when a manager is able to foresee things in proper perspective, he can plan his activities to suit the future needs. Under such circumstances all his programmes can be properly implemented so that he can achieve the company's objectives successfully.

Creativity leads to Success

Those with wisdom have everything.
Fools with everything have nothing.

Kural 430

Everyone wants to think of something new to solve a problem no one else can solve, offer a valuable idea no one else conceived. And every business person wants to encourage its employees to have the next great idea.

So when a business offers its employees a bonus for innovative ideas, a flood of great, original thoughts should come pouring in. Right?

We think that creativity, like any other task, can be bought and sold. But creativity is not the same as hard work and effort, it requires genuine inspiration.

Thus, creativity comes not in exchange for money or rewards but when we focus earnest attention on something, it comes from within.

Japan Railways (East) had the contract to build a bullet train between Tokyo and Nagano to be put in place in time for the 1998 Winter Olympics. Unfortunately, tunnels built by the company through the mountains kept filling with water. The company brought in a team of engineers, who were highly paid to come up with the best solution. The engineers analysed the problems and drew up an extensive set of plans to build an expensive drain and a system of aquaducts to divert the water out of the tunnels.

A thirsty maintenance worker one day came up with a different solution when he bent over and took a large swallow of the tunnel water. It tasted great, better than the bottled water he had in his lunch pail.

He told his boss they should bottle it and sell it as premium mineral water.

Thus was born Oshimizu bottled water business, which the railroad sells from vending machines on its platforms and has expanded to selling by home delivery.

A huge cost was transformed into a huge profit, all by looking at the situation differently.

Experiments offering money in exchange for innovative solutions to problems find that monetary rewards are unrelated to the capacity of people to offer original ideas. Instead, creativity is most frequently the product of genuine interest in the problem and a faith that creativity will be personally appreciated by superiors.

Never do for the sake of doing

Men may pass all tests, yet they vary
in their ways of discharging duty.

Kural 514

Certain jobs require a distinct personality. There is no point in pursuing a job in communications if we are not an extroverted person who loves to interact with people. Personalities are like shoe sizes. They are not subject to our choice or preference, but they can be occasionally fudged with uncomfortable consequences.

It is neither an accomplishment nor a fault to acknowledge that some people can speak before large audiences and be exhilarated by the experience while others would be petrified. Some people can study an equation for years and be fascinated by it, and others would long for human interaction and variety.

Jean Deer is a photographer. He loves his job passionately. He has taken hundreds of children's portraits, and he is well acquainted with all the tricks of the trade to make the baby smile.

'When it's over, everyone—me, the parents, and the children—are exhausted, but that's usually a good sign.'

Jean found that getting babies to flash their smiles wasn't

the only way to get a great picture and that a grumpy baby was just another source of inspiration. 'I was taking a photo once of this infant who literally wanted nothing to do with me. He would not look up, just stared at the floor.' Jean got down on the floor with him, took the picture from a perspective he had never used before, and wound up with one of the best pictures he'd ever taken.

The job requires two major traits, Jean believes. 'Not everyone can just hang out a sling and call himself a photographer; it's all a matter of being patient and energetic and then capturing the right moment.'

Even as people experience different phases of their lives, including career and family changes, their underlying personality remains constant after attaining the age of sixteen.

Self Esteem

Men of greatness do rare deeds
in proper and perfect ways.

Kural 975

All of us will suffer blows to our self-esteem when we fail. Regardless of how strong our beliefs are, negative outcomes will shake us.

When events undermine our self-esteem, we must have faith in ourself that it is unquestionable. This faith in our integrity and our humanity will survive any attack based on failures. It will give us something to start from, as we rebuild our self-esteem.

Peter Shane is the Dean of the University of Pittsburgh Law School. He tells his graduates that after learning law, and even achieving confidence in themselves, their education is not complete. You will need more. You will need courage, especially if you are going to be a leader in the settings where you live, work, and worship. If you advocate change, you will have to understand that there is no change so small that it threatens no one. The dean tells students that the world is filled with temptations to cut corners and to take the path of least resistance. To overcome, they must see their actions as exemplary to others. There is no greater measure of the example we provide as a leader, as a lawyer, as a citizen, or as a parent than the decency with which we treat other human beings. This is true whether we are dealing with a friend or foe, colleague or opponent, superior or subordinate.

Self-esteem by itself may not predict success; with a little bit of imagination and smartness it brings success.

Set Reasonable Targets

The whole world is his who acts
at the right time and place.

Kural 484

Of course, we can never measure ourselves against concepts and opinions because they are too abstract to define. Thus, we can't say whether we're making progress or we need to change.

Then we have to define our goals, and define our plans to attain them.

Nancy is a consultant who works with small business concerns. Her job is to help small business owners develop a map for their future.

She meets her clients once a month to talk about where they are and where they are going. Too many small business owners spend time dealing with one crisis after another, rather than managing their business.

The toughest hurdle, Nancy says, is just getting started in setting concrete goals so that the business can serve the long term needs of the owner rather than the owner spending time serving short-term needs of the business.

People who construct their goals are 50 per cent more likely to feel confident and they will attain their goals

Climbing a tree beyond the tip of a branch
will be the end of life very much.

Kural 476

People on top want to stay on top. It's not surprising. But people who want to experience an incredible success wind up yearning for that experience long after it is gone.

Let us set our sights, not on reaching an ultimate moment that will quickly come and even more quickly go, but on reaching a level of achievement that is both satisfying and sustainable. Upstate New York florist Patricia Woyshner had been in the business for forty years.

She was selling flowers to tens of thousands in the area and even received one of the best assignments a florist could hope for, decorating the White House for the Christmas season.

Despite the excitement, Patricia's focus remained steady on her day-to-day concerns. She realised that while she knew everything about flowers, she was not an expert in marketing her business. 'All my education was related to the floral industry. I realised that I should try to learn from other industries because they face problems that are very similar to ours.'

Patricia attended business school seminars designed to help her attract repeat business. Patricia reported, the classes helped, her customer base was up, and even the White House called and asked her to decorate again.

Make a Change When You Have to

An inefficient minister will always fail
to finish even a plan designed well.

Kural 640

How many times do you finish something even though you wish you'd never started it?

We clean our plates even if the carrots are overcooked because they are there and we've already started. We do this even though we would never seek overcooked carrots and wouldn't want them if anyone offered them to us.

We sit in the movie theatre and keep watching the movie when we think it's terrible, even though under no circumstances would we say yes, if someone asked ,'would you like to watch forty five minutes of an awful movie?'

We do the same thing when we continue a project that is off target. We keep going because we've already started, not because it makes any sense to continue what we're doing. Be prepared to stop, based not on what you've already invested but on what you stand to gain by continuing.

Brad runs a high-tech security firm and sees the insides and the decision making process of all kinds of companies. The most amazing part of this business is the number of times you'll hear that a business is concerned that their security is inadequate but that they can't make a change right now because they're already paying for another system.

Brad tells them, well, if you're already paying for another system that doesn't work, you're not really paying for security. He adds, I really question when management teams refuse to make a change, even after they acknowledge the need for it, because they don't want to look bad for having made the wrong decision the first time, or they don't want to waste the money paying twice for something. When I hear that I wonder if they can ever adapt to their environment, or if they will go down in flames because they had to follow the plan no matter what happens.

In experimental settings, people rate the feasibility of continuing the development of a new product, based more on its nearness to completion than on the likelihood of the product producing a profit.

Jealousy of Peers

Waging a war without well thought out plans
is to rear the foes in vantage fields.

Kural 465

On the path to success, we may sometimes confront situations in which we must directly compete with someone and our victory will create bitterness. Even more frequently, our success will cause others to compare themselves to us and to react with jealousy at our ability.

Take comfort in the knowledge that it is not a personal attack on us, but instead, a sincere but unpleasant form of flattery.

'Every year, I spend less time talking around the water cooler', says Sheila. 'As we advance up the corporate ladder, a lot of people begin to think of us as enemy.'

Sheila struggled with the implications of her rapid rise through the ranks of the financial services company where she works. 'At the same time, we can't sit around wishing away success, so that our co-workers will like us again', she adds.

The best advice on the matter came from her father, who toiled for forty-five years without achieving the advancements his daughter had in less than ten. He said to Sheila, 'Treat everyone with respect, and don't treat anyone, above or below you, based on their station. Eventually, that respect will come back'. Six in ten top managers report that they have lost friendships among co-workers who were not promoted as fast as they were.

True Leadership

Firmness in action is but robust mind.
All others are not of that kind.

Kural 661

True leadership strengthens the followers. It is a process of teaching, setting an example, and empowering others.

If you seek to lead, your ability will ultimately be measured in the successes of those around you.

This isn't a job for individuals working alone; this is a job for a team. One has to be very fair to the others and then they get the message that they have to be that way to every citizen they interact with.

The way chiefs get into trouble is by showing favouritism. When the top goes bad, then the rest of the organisation goes bad. But when the top sets the right tone, then everybody can follow that lead.

Despite the power we associate with the idea of a leader, 93 per cent of those who actually lead an organisation view themselves at least partially as a 'servant of the people' in their organisation.

The tendency to start more and more without serious intent or ability to complete is totally unbecoming of a true executive. The very purpose of the existence of an executive is to accomplish tasks. There is no useful purpose served by tasks which are just well begun and half done. Persons who do not have the zeal to complete are not executives. But a true executive, worth his salt, must possess the passion and determination to annihilate any obstacle that he might encounter. After all, nobody is interested in hearing excuses, they only want to get things done.

Modesty gives a unique place among colleagues and subordinates. Grace shown to those in the lower rung is a sterling human quality which moulds a perfect leader. All these qualities can help him in motivating his whole team and obtaining the support of his colleagues and seniors in order to achieve the objectives with ease. Hence, a leader with all these five qualities succeeds in all his endeavours, though endless they may seem.

Domestic Relations

DOMESTIC RELATIONS impacts work and office administration. The first human relations are relations within a family. All who want to improve human relations should have a good understanding in the family. 'Charity begins at home.' Similarly the best of public relations has its roots at home.

A man leading domestic life is he
who supports the virtuous three.

Kural 41

The three mentioned herein are the brahmachari or student, hermit, dweller in the forest and the absolute ascetic. Therefore, in order to uphold a glorious family life, he has to maintain good relations with all these three. Thiruvalluvar shows the way for a family man to maintain cordial relationship with society at large.

Ancestors, god, self, kindred and guests
are a family man's chief interests.

Kural 43

The two good qualities *Thirukkural* has been advocating throughout are love and virtue. Christ made this plea to all human beings 'Love thy neighbour'. Before loving the neighbour, it is necessary to love your own family members. The other quality is virtue. Virtue not only improves human relations within the family but also enhances the prestige of the family in the society.

Essentials of Married life

We cannot expect love to be automatic. It has to be cherished. It has to be nurtured by being together. It can be kept alive by having fun with each other. One should not permit the pressures of daily life to turn one's wedlock into a series of botherations. The couple should remember the things they enjoyed together at the beginning of their married life. They can nourish the marital life by giving support to the ideas and efforts of the spouse.

Let us turn to one *Thirukkural* couplet which explains the love between a husband and wife.

The association of the soul and the body
is the fruit of the life of love only

Kural 73

Love between a husband and wife is like a bond between a soul and a body. If such a bond exists between husband

and wife, they will definitely take pains to live together for years. The husband should try to learn about the wife. One's goals, values, concerns and hopes should be revealed to the others so that the other spouse respects them without any disregard. This is a basic necessity for the marital success. The bond mentioned in *Thirukkural* is developed if we know such things.

Virtue

Thirukkural emphasises virtue as one of the good qualities which nurtures family relations.

Honesty: The foremost quality of virtue is honesty. Honesty is expressed through word and deed. If one is not actually satisfied with the other in any field he/she should express the same politely. Similarly what he expects should also be honestly expressed. Hence honesty as a virtue has to be cherished by both the partners to maintain harmonious marital relations.

Envy: Another virtuous quality is to avoid jealousy. At times though it may seem natural for one to become jealous it is necessary that it should not be nourished. It should be nipped in the bud. Thiruvalluvar has stated,

No one has prospered through jealousy.
Nor the unenvious have lost prosperity.

Kural 170

Hence we may see that not being jealous is a great virtue *Thirukkural* has advocated. We often see that in a number of cases marital relations have been spoilt out of jealousy and the partners reach a point of no return. Again *Thirukkural* stresses the evils of envy as below:

Fortune herself will desert the envious
and direct her sister to the envious.

Kural 167

A man will be destroyed by his own envy, even if enemies spare him.

Therefore if a family has to prosper it is quite necessary that jealousy is not given room. Jealousy can be eliminated if the couples are prepared to talk it out in case of doubts.

Apart from jealousy other negative qualities should also be eliminated as the above process is basis for virtue.

Envy, greed, wrath and evil words.
It's virtue to shun these ills.

Kural 35

The other three negative qualities the couples should avoid are greed, anger and harsh words. We are well aware that greed is the basis for other bad qualities. If one eliminates this bad quality, he can raise himself to great heights.

Greed

An ideal wife maintains dignity of home
and lives within her husband's income

Kural-51

Any human being has got every right to desire to own something. Whatever may be one's desire, it should be reasonable. One's ambitions should be well within his limits. To like to attain something beyond reach or what is not one's due is really greed, and one should take necessary precautionary measures to eliminate them. Greed ultimately leads to destruction.

We can easily see in some families the couples, either of them or both, spending lavishly beyond their income which in turn lead to huge debts beyond repayment. They may have to mortgage or sell their properties for clearing their debts. Such things create not only a storm in marital relations but also destroy the whole family.

Anger

Fire of anger that guts all who draw near it
burns kinship, the life-boat.

Kural 306

Anger is another negative quality which spoils good relations. This couplet clearly teaches us that anger spoils one who sports it. Apart from that, it burns the kinship. No relative would like to maintain good relations with one who has angry disposition. Anger burns the kinship and also burns the marital relations.

Anger may be natural reaction on certain occasions. Every human being may feel angry now and then. One who knows how to control anger and makes use of this negative quality to ensure a positive result is an expert in building relations. Immediate reaction of a human being who gets angry is sudden outburst of harsh words.

A simple method some experts suggest is to count upto ten when one gets angry. The counterproductive emotion and anger spoils all types of relations.

Harsh Words

Is there any greater foe than anger
which kills joy and laughter?

Kural 304

Another negative quality one should avoid in order to maintain a cordial relation is the use of harsh words.

Knowing well the pleasure of sweet words
why cast bitter ones at others?

Kural 99

Harsh words are often spoken by one due to envy, anger, arrogance or even inadvertently. One should take special efforts to control his tongue, especially if he is in the habit of using harsh words.

Even a single evil word will bury all good things. Whatever good has been achieved in so many days, months and years can be easily spoiled by some harsh words even inadvertently spoken. Hence it is all the more necessary that one should guard his tongue lest he may suffer later.

Minor arguments on some trivial things may sometime turn into bitter arguments. Tolerance and understanding the other side can prevent such bitter arguments. Marriage is not always fifty fifty. At times it is eighty twenty and sometime later it is twenty eighty. The couple who understand this will never permit bitter arguments.

The wife may suggest the purchase of a brand new product introduced in the market. As the husband keeps quiet, the wife may accuse him of indecision. The husband may say that she is a spendthrift. The argument may go on leaving the subject behind. The arguments develop only because both think that their images or rather egos should be defended. Cultivating humility helps in eliminating ego problems.

Humility

Humility is surely a great virtue for one and all.
To the wealthy it is another wealth above all.

Kural 125

As suggested by Thiruvalluvar, both the husband and wife should cultivate humility, control their egos and avoid harsh words to cultivate better relations.

Vain words spoken in public are worse
than wrongs done to mates.

Kural 192

When sweet words are able to achieve so much why should not the couple use them and improve relations.

Love is one of the fine qualities to maintain cordial marital relations. To keep the love alive proper conjugal relations are quite necessary. Thiruvalluvar has also advocated the same through a number of *Thirukkural* couplets. By courting and nurturing, sexual relations can be improved. Even meaningful glances and looks help in expressing love. They can be added later with words.

She looked; as I looked, her head drooped.
It resembled watering our love-plant.

Kural 1093

Though, like a stranger, she speaks harshly,
her words are soon found to be friendly.

Kural 1096

Couples should develop love not only by looks but also through such loving words. Sexual desire can be further kindled by physical contacts like touching and embracing. Here we see a *Thirukkural* couplet describing an embrace of the beloved.

Who love and are loved with loving care
gain the seedless fruit of love so rare.

Kural 1191

What feast shall I give this dream now
that brings my lover's word of love?

Kural 1211

Pleasures of Family Life

These couplets indicate the priority that lovemaking deserves. Now let us see how the relations with children also can be improved. Children are the real wealth of the couple. Their wealth is measured by their deeds.

Children deserve the attention of their parents as real wealth. They should be brought up in such a way that they perform good deeds as their worth is measured only by their deeds.

No doubt that the parents are fond of their babies. Mother and father take pride in their babies and even in their babbles.

Who have not heard their babies' babble
say flute and lute are delightful.

Kural 66

When we think of babies as exhibition of all that we wish, we should take enough care in bringing them up. Parents have high expectations of their children. A number of *Thirukkural* couplets explain the pleasure of the parents, when their expectations of their children fructify.

Of all blessings we know nothing is greater
than begetting children wiser.

Kural 61

When their children grow up wise as well as virtuous, the joy of the parents knows no bound as it is the highest form of bliss they could get. Of course these things will not come automatically. The parents have to work hard for it. They should synchronise well with the tunes of their children in order to develop them into successful adults.

Father's responsibility to his son lies
in placing him ahead of scholars.

Kural 67

Unless one forms part of the creamy layer, he can't occupy the front bench in wisemen's council. As such, the parents have to work for the same.

Let us see some tips to make the children wise and virtuous. It is necessary that children should develop independence, self-confidence, self respect and competence. They are the basic attributes of mental health. These can be cultivated by doing chores. This not only helps in getting the domestic chores completed as desired but also helps the child understand the spirit of cooperation by working together to attain common goals. Competent adults have been brought up that way.

This habit should be cultivated at an early stage. Children should never be overworked. Then instead of working for pleasure they may view them as drudgery. What is possible for their age, they may be asked to do. Such efforts improve the relations of children with their parents because the parents perform the role of friends, philosophers and guides and take the opportunity to appreciate and encourage the children even at an early age to develop their skills.

Some couples, especially fathers, are reluctant to compliment their children. They feel that praise will spoil their children by inducing an inflated ego. But actually that is not the case. Praising the children whenever due helps them develop their skills and improve their behaviour.

Whenever a child tries hard despite failure or whenever a child shows some improvement the child needs to be appreciated even though it has not achieved cent percent success. Such a child who receives compliments whenever due becomes self-confident and maintains poise. It ensures emotional integration with other children and also with their own parents.

Not being one-sided like an even balance
is an ornament to the wise.

Kural 118

The above *Thirukkural* clearly indicates that the parents should be well poised in their approach to their children and their rivalry. Such an approach as we saw earlier will ensure the overall development of their children.

Value merit of men with morals and sagacity
and secure their amity.

Kural 441

How lucky is a man whose own parents can become his friends, philosopher and guide.

To have men greater than oneself as relatives
and follow them is the chief of powers.

Kural 444

Such being the case it is not only our bounden duty but also a benign act to keep our parents with us and have their advice. It is quite essential that we should take care of our parents, improve our relations with them and keep them in good health and cheer.

Son's duty to father is to make others wonder
what penance got such a son to the father

Kural 70

Social Relations

SOCIAL RELATIONS play a vital role in making a man successful in life and enjoy quality life. One who can maintain cordial domestic relations has got every chance to improve and maintain cordial social relations and public relations. Thiruvalluvar has got a lot to guide us with his *Thirukkural* couplets.

Love and Affection
Love and affection towards other fellow beings are reiterated by Thiruvalluvar in a number of couplets.

Love begets the life of love for others
and amity of excellence it yields.

Kural 74

Love Eliminates Vices
Love and affection shown to others are basic traits in a human being which brings forth friendship par excellence.

The love and affection which radiate from a human being make other people take interest in him. As flies are attracted by the light, human beings are attracted by friendship which is the ultimate culmination of human relations.

'Love helps only virtue', say the unwise.
It also guards us from all evils.

Kural 76

Love is a very fine quality which makes one lead a virtuous life. One who leads a virtuous life is always considered as a guide. More predominant to human senses are vices. Love and affection of a human being apart from making him lead a virtuous life also helps him to eliminate vices. Others are also inspired by his example with the guidance of a loving man. They are also able to lead a virtuous life. The first step in leading a virtuous life lies in elimination of vices. Once vices are eliminated and virtuous life is established we can maintain the best of social relations.

The loveless grab all for themselves.
The loving give even their bones.

Kural 72

This is the essence of social life. Love is a selfless quality. Those who do not have any affection towards others are generally selfish. Whatever they think, whatever they talk and whatever they do centre only around them and their belongings.

They do not care about others' lives, ambitions and aspirations. But it is not the case with those who develop love and affection towards others. Naturally, they are selfless.

They care for others. They are prepared to help others even without asking. Their thoughts, speeches and deeds centre on others. Such people are indeed a boon to the society as they are responsible for the best of human relations not only between themselves but also between various other members of the society.

Christ said to people, 'Love Thy Neighbour as Thyself'. Loving one's neighbour is not only a virtuous quality but also a lesson in social life.

Hospitality is another good quality and advocated by Thiruvalluvar for all of us. Let us look to the *Thirukkural* couplet on this subject.

Keeping home and guarding riches
is to help and entertain guests.

Kural 81

This couplet strangely states that the idea of running a home itself is to welcome the guests and attend to their needs.

Be Hospitable

Being hospitable to the guests is considered to be the duty of the people to the society.

Goddess of fortune gladly dwells in that house
where guests are greeted with smiling face.

Kural 84

The first and foremost attribute of hospitability is a cheerful and smiling disposition. Guests have to be welcomed with a smiling face. The smile is the expression of the generosity of the heart. Goddess of the wealth bestows special affection on such hospitable people and would like to stay with them. Thus by advocating hospitality as an essential quality of social life, *Thirukkural* ensures improvement of social relations through hospitality.

Another important method for improvement of human relations often repeated in *Thirukkural* is speaking sweet words.

Gratitude

One more quality which raises a man high in society is his sense of gratitude. Here in various couplets Thiruvalluvar stresses the importance of doing good things to others unsolicited and in hours of need. He also wants us to be grateful to those who do something good for us. Hence the importance of both sides of the coin of doing good is explained in his couplets.

Even heaven and earth will be a scant reward
for a help from one never rewarded.

Kural 101

Two great things we have heard about are the earth and heaven. Even though someone has not helped us so far if we offer them good help, ie. necessary help he is in need of, the help rendered by us is worthier than earth and heaven put together. In other words when you help a man who has not helped you so far, it is the greatest help rendered.

Next Thiruvalluvar stresses the importance of timely help.

Timely Help

A timely help, though small in worth
is greater than the earth.

Kural 102

What is the use of offering help to somebody if it is not done in the hour of need. Help has to be offered immediately at the time of need so that the suffering of the other man is stalled and the hardship, eliminated. Then only it will be of real help to the individual. To overcome the timely help may be small but it is effective. Thiruvalluvar says such timely help is greater than the world itself.

Another important point one should note when helping others is that there should not be any expectations on the part of the helper.

Call that a gift to needy men thou dost dispense.
All else is void of good, seeking for recompense.

Kural 221

Most of us would have enjoyed the grandeur of the ocean. When an individual helps others without any expectations ie. without caring about what the one receives will do in turn it is really a culmination of grandeur of humanism. Such an act even outweighs the ocean in its greatness.

'All for one and one for all', said Lenin. When every member of the society thinks so, it will be the highest civilised society. That is what Thiruvalluvar has also intimated. Let us see the other side of the coin. How one who receives help should think and act has also been explained by Thiruvalluvar.

Irrespective of his quantum of help, small in size of a millet, the receiver will consider it as big as a palm tree, when its use is meritorious.

Though the help received is millet small,
the worthy deem it palm-tree tall.

Kural 104

One face of it may seem that the help rendered by an individual is very small, but it will look different to one who is in need of it. The beneficiaries are really thankful along these lines.

The same point is explained in another couplet.

Help given is not measured by its measure.
It depends on the worth of the receiver.

Kural 105

Some people may think that as the help they are expected to do is very small, they can as well stay away from it as those who are in need of it can somehow manage. Such impressions should be removed from our minds. However small may be the help, one should come forward to do it because it will be something great for the beneficiary. It is the gainer's worth and pleasure which decides the necessity of help.

Forgetting the good is no good but it's good
to forget at once what is no good.

Kural 108

This is an advice to the recipient. Whenever one receives a help from others he should not forget it. But on the other hand if anybody fails to help him or does any harm he should not brood over it. Forgive and forget should be the motto. When members of a society develop such an attitude, there is no doubt the relationship will be very cordial. The same point is again brought forth in another couplet.

Even a death-like harm becomes nullified
at the thought of one favour obtained.

Kural 109

It is only a harm (a wrong thing done), which should be forgotten, on the other hand even a single help should be remembered thankfully forever.

Self-control

One more important quality explained in *Thirukkural* is humility and self-control.

Self-control will place one among gods.
Lack of it sinks one into a life of evils.

Kural 121

Self-control is such an exalted virtue that it leads the persons who cultivate the virtue to heaven. Thiruvalluvar is equally sure that indulgence in all sorts of activities without any control will lead personality in the opposite direction and land him in hell.

Self-control guided by wisdom
fetches everlasting fame.

Kural 123

One should be wise enough to control oneself. If he is able to exercise such control, name and fame will come to him, even if he does not work for them and if he does not have any such expectations.

Name and fame in this world during his life and a safe place in the heavens are the requirements of a human being. Self-control can bring both. Then why don't we practice the same?

Restrain five senses in one birth like a tortoise.
You'll be guarded in all seven births.

Kural 126

Controlling of senses may be a difficult task for a human being. But for a man to lead a really happy and cherished life controlling of sense is very important. A man who is able to control his senses can lead a happy life not only during this birth but also in all the seven births says Thiruvalluvar.

Another good quality suggested by Thiruvalluvar is good conduct and behavior. These qualities should be taught in every school to enable our children to become good citizens of the country. Let us see what is taught through *Thirukkural* couplets.

Character

The wise can learn the forgotten lore again.
But loss of good conduct leads to ruin.

Kural 134

We would have heard of the proverb 'When character is lost everything is lost.' Good conduct is part and parcel of good character. Whatever you have read even if you forget you may recall it once again by referring to the books or consulting those who know. But how about good conduct? Once it is lost, it is lost forever, leaving a blemish behind. As such one should take care to nurture good conduct.

Good conduct ever brings great honour.
Bad conduct ends in great dishonour.

Kural 137

A man of exemplary conduct is considered to be noble by the society whereas a man whose conduct is questionable is viewed upon with disgrace by the same society. As the conduct exalts the individual in society, one should take care to cultivate good manners and behaviour.

Just as the jealous have no prosperity
the indecent have no dignity.

Kural 135

Those who are envious are not liked by the society. But the condition of the people whose behavior is bad is still worse. They are not tolerated by others. Their esteem in other's views goes down. Even the first impression they make on others mind is no good. Then how can they manage to win others' hearts?

Noble character is the seed of righteousness.
Ignoble character brings ills endless.

Kural 138

The effects of good and bad behaviour have been defined emphatically in this couplet. Conduct is generally integration of one's behaviour during a particular period.

It is watched and estimated on a continuous basis. Good conduct paves the way for earning the blessings of elders and those who count in the society. But the effect of bad conduct is immediate and opposite. It brings only evil things. Hence it is the duty of every good citizen to cultivate good manners and behaviour worthy of exemplary conduct. Let us go to the last couplet on good conduct.

Be in Harmony with the World

Who cannot live in harmony with the world
though learned, are fools indeed.

Kural 140

This is a very good lesson for all those who want to make a mark in society. One may be a great scholar. He might have read a lot of books. He might have heard lots of things. All his studies and education will be of any use only if he knows how to live as desired by the cream of the society.

If he is not able to live as desired by the society he is considered to be an ignorant man even though he might have earned a doctorate.

This is an oft-quoted *Thirukkural* couplet. This teaches a man that he should learn to live in a practical world and not merely in a theoretical world.

Learn to Forgive

One more important quality explained by Thiruvalluvar is forgiveness. This supreme quality boosts the image of an individual. It gives him inner peace.

To bear with others' evil is a good trait.
Better it is to forget it.

Kural 152

There is an adage 'forgive and forget'. The same policy has been advocated by Thiruvalluvar long back. It is very difficult for a man to tolerate insults heaped on him. Many a war has broken out in this world because some heads of governments could not tolerate what they see as insults. Therefore it is very difficult for a man to put up with insults. However difficult it may be it is necessary for a man who likes to grow in status, to forgive insults. Once he forgives the insults hurled at him he should be able to forget them. Then only he will have mental peace and can concentrate on the good work to be done. Let us see another couplet.

Who punish the offenders are despised.
Who forbear are esteemed like gold.

Kural 155

This couplet reiterates the policy of 'Forgive and forget.' A man is a social being. Society does not-hold in esteem one who wants to wreak vengeance on others. Hence it is not a desirable quality as the part of a man who wants to have a name in society by improving social relations. But if a man observes patience even though things go against his liking and even if he is insulted, that is considered a golden quality. It brings him regard and respect whenever necessary just like reserve gold fetches one money whenever required.

Be tolerant

Conquer men who do evils by arrogance
simply by your tolerance.

Kural 158

By 'Tit for Tat' we cannot win. That policy will create a vicious vortex from which you can't easily come out. Hence it is better to forebear any evil things done to you. That quality of forbearance will not only raise your image to those around you in the society but also with even those who did you harm. This is the path shown by our great spiritual leaders. Saint Thiruvalluvar also shows that to us towards salvation.

Better are they who endure bitter insults
than those who fast and do penance.

Kural 160

It is general religious ritual for us to fast. It is considered to be a form of penance. It helps us a lot in improving our physical as well as mental health. But bearing the offence done to us by others is considered to be greater than the penance of fasting. Fasting is undertaken by us of our own accord. As it is performed with our own mental support we can fast successfully. On the other hand the forbearing of evil done to us by others is rather difficult. We have to prepare our mind for this by cultivating patience. When we achieve this catalyst forbearance in the eyes of the society we are looked upon as people of greater virtue than those who fast and do similar forms of penance. Hence forgiving and forbearance are indeed the best forms of penance for human beings. Let us pass on to another virtue recommended by Thiruvalluvar. It is avoiding jealousy.

Be not Envious

Of all the goodness nothing can equal
being free from envy of one and all.

Kural 162

Perhaps human tendency is to be jealous of those who are more fortunate in life. If one wants to improve and ensure proper relations with other members of the society this quality of envy should be eliminated. But there are certain people who are not envious by nature. This is an excellent virtue Nature has bestowed on them. Though one may have excelled in a number of fields the excellence of non-envy excels all such excellence and is indeed par excellence.

Having thus seen the positive aspects of non-envy let us see the negative aspects of envy through one *Thirukkural.*

Who know that envy causes misery
will do no wrong out of envy.

Kural 164

If one commits some offence on others because of envy what will happen to him? From those evils only woes will throng the offender. Keeping this in their mind, wise people neither envy nor nurse envy of others.

Kin of those who envy charity to others
perish without food and clothes.

Kural 166

When somebody receives a present, a gift or a prize there are some people who aspire for the same but are unable to get it. Some such people become envious. What is the result of this envy? That can never be positive. Because of envy such people suffer without food and clothes as it is a curse on the society of such people. As society does not respect such people they suffer for want of help and support from the society. As such in order to gain the respect of the society and improve social relations it is necessary to shun envy, without any reservations.

Covet Not

Another point stressed in *Thirukkural* is avoiding coveteousness. One should never try to abdicate the wealth of other individuals or public property.

Covet not wealth gained through greed.
For its fruits rarely do good.

Kural 177

Society is not going to glorify one who is covetous as it is one of the bitter vices. As such it is better one shuns covetousness. Then only he can have a chance of restoring even lost glory.

Thoughtless coveting leads to destruction.
Greedless pride brings distinction.

Kural 180

This couplet clearly indicates that one who shuns desires wins over the society whereas covetous people are ruined to the core. 'Spread no rumour. Believe no rumour'. This is rather a new adage. But on the other hand *Thirukkural* has been preaching against all types of slanders from time immemorial.

Who cannot foster friends through pleasing words
lose friendship through slandering ones.

Kural 187

Slander Is Shameful

What is the use of slander? It can only break the kinship between people. Therefore it is antisocial. It is not liked by the people. On the other hand if one uses sweet words he can create friendship. He can unite other people in friendship. Those who want to improve social relations should keep themselves away from all sorts of slander. Campaign and use only pleasing words. How can one desist from slander? Here also *Thirukkural* guides us in inimitable style.

If everyone sees his faults as he sees others'
will any evil ever fall on living beings?

Kural 190

Introspect Yourself

If every man can identify his own defects he will be engaged in rectifying his defects. He will neither have the time nor inclination to spread slander about others. This is a very good advice to human beings in general.

Vain Speaking

Apart from slander a number of people indulge in speaking vain words. Such vain talks also spoil all human relations.

Through a number of couplets, Thiruvalluvar speaks about the evil effects of vain speaking.

One's vain and crude words before an assembly
remove one's gains and goodness simply.

Kural 194

One who wants to be a respectable member of the society and who wants to be held in esteem should make it a point to desist from speaking vain words especially before an assembly. One has nothing to gain from this vain talk. But he will lose whatever he has gained so far. When he loses respect in society what else will remain?

Throw them or it may be a rare show of vanity. On the other hand giving the poor and needy, services to correct the social imbalance, is a good virtue.

People on the earth who are satisfied regarding the basic needs of their families will be striving for name and fame in the society. Thiruvalluvar is prepared to guide them in this respect also.

Name and Fame

The only benefit in life is glory
that comes of charity.

Kural 231

This is in fact a continuation of the ideas expressed in the previous couplets. The virtue of giving brings fame from society for an individual. This couplet also describes fame as the greatest gain for human beings.

Fame in fall and life in doom
are only to men of wisdom.

Kural 235

Rise and fall is common for people living in a society. Even though one falls from his status he will not fall from his stature in society (if he is a virtuous man). Such people will be living in the hearts of others even after their deaths. Such is their fame.

Enter a field and build up repute.
If not, it's better to enter not.

Kural 236

Once a man is popular when he is liked by the people of his society he will live with fame. If he is not liked by the people and his relations in the society are bad, he cannot earn a good name.

These couplets stress the necessity for human beings to lead such a social life that they earn name and fame in the society. Compassion is another virtue exalted by Thiruvalluvar for the people to lead a fruitfull life in the society.

Wealth of wealth is the wealth of kindness.
Worldly wealth even the mean possess.

Kural 241

Even an ordinary person can amass wealth by hook or by crook. Therefore such wealth is not considered to be a real wealth by the members of the society. What is the real wealth? It is the graceful outlook on others in society. If one cultivates such a virtue he is considered to be a man who has amassed real wealth.

Mercy on All Beings

Men of mercy who guard all beings
are free from fear of evils.

Kural 244

If one cultivates the virtue of mercy in all other human beings he need not be afraid of sins. Mercy will see that he does not commit any sin as it is a basic virtue which avoids any sign of sinful thoughts from the mind, when all sinful thoughts are eliminated at the first trace one need not be afraid of sins.

The poor may perhaps flourish some day.
But the cruel prosper not any day.

Kural 248

One who does not have any money can also prosper one day or other if he is able to earn it on a sunny day. But it is not the case with graceless people. When the graceful blossom can spread their fragrance, the graceless are a waste as they can never bloom.

Imagine yourself facing the stronger
while oppressing the weaker.

Kural 250

This couplet is a very good lesson for those who offend people weaker than themselves without mercy whatever may be the reasons.

When a stronger man mercilessly attempts to offend a weaker person, he should think of his pathetic position when he is shivering in front of a rather stronger person than himself. Thereby he can never decide to commit offences on anybody in the society.

This is an apt lesson to all of us for living harmoniously in a society.

Thieves have no Morals

Another virtue hailed by Thiruvalluvar for living with pride in society is absence of fraud in one's thoughts.

One should guard the mind against theft
if one wants to escape contempt.

Kural 281

If one clears his mind from all thoughts of frauds with the help of clear conscience, the society will never reproach him. He will live with a name and fame in the society.

Stolen wealth may appear a gain
but it will result in limitless ruin.

Kural 283

Even though one may get some money or some other thing belonging to others or some common property by deceitful means it will not last forever. It will go as fast as it came and ultimately he will come to grief due to this ruin.

The blackest craft of basest fraud is not found
in men with measured wisdom sound.

Kural 287

A wise man knows the limits of every sphere in life. Such a man never permits in his mind thoughts of fraud and deceit. Naturally he is hailed as a sagacious man in society.

Be Truthful

Another quality stressed by Thiruvalluvar in his inimitable *Thirukkural* couplets is veracity, ie. speaking Truth.

What is Truth? If the question be.
It's speech with words evil-free.

Kural 291

What we talk should be harmless. It should not bring evils to those around us or beyond. Such words are called Truth by Thiruvalluvar. When people realise the same and speak only evil free words the evils will be eliminated from the society which will raise to new heights. His definition of Truth is further clarified in another couplet.

Even untruth has the stamp of truthfulness
if it brings good sans harmfulness.

Kural 292

How can anybody be fictitious to Truth? Is it correct? Even an ordinary man knows it is not truth. Then the great Thiruvalluvar advises like this. The second line of the couplet clears all our doubts. The lies or falsehood may also be kept at par with truth if such utterances can cause goodness to people without any harm. After all the main objective of speaking and doing is to bring good by conquering evil. When it is achieved by talking some fiction there is nothing wrong in it.

Who remains true to his conscience
lives forever in all noble hearts.

Kural 294

This couplet gives a fairly good idea of the effect of serving the course of truth. One who talks truth and acts truthfully improves his relations in the society. His relations are so cordial that he lives in the loving hearts of one and all in the society. That is what one born as a human expects.

If you observe non-lying and non-lying only
you needn't practise other virtues really.

Kural 297

This couplet again reiterates how a man who is truthful and who never lies is held by the society. Such a man is virtuous as truth is a basic virtue which gives all praise for such a virtuous man.

Anger is an Enemy

One more virtue which is brought to light in *Thirukkural* couplets is controlling anger. For one who wants to improve in social relations, controlling anger is an important factor.

Restrain anger where it would have effect.
Elsewhere, curbed or not, it matters not.

Kural 301

Anger against the weaker people is considered to be a sin in the society. On the other hand if you are angry with the strong and mighty you are going to lose all such anger since they are only a futile exercise.

Is there any greater foe than anger
which kills joy and laughter?

Kural 304

A smile is a messenger of good will. Like one lamp lights another, one smile induces smile on another's face and it spreads joy and cheer throughout. A smile is a medium which improves relations. It is symbolic of harmony.

The anger kills such a smile on one's face. By killing smile it also eliminates joy and cheer. As such it is a social evil to be eliminated at any cost.

After all human beings are social beings. They want to cherish their friendship with others. They also want their kinship to flourish. Such being the desire of human beings they should not indulge themselves in rage. Rage is described as fatal because it kills one's friendship with his companions. It also destroys his kinship with his relatives. As such in order to maintain harmonious relations with one's friends and relatives it is necessary one should give up anger.

Company of the Wise

Thiruvalluvar expects people to be wise enough to make their social life happy and fruitful. He has stressed the same in a number of couplets.

Friendship of the great without wax or wane
is wisdom true and sane.

Kural 425

Wise people are always conscious of the society. They act according to the wishes of the society by befriending the cream of the society. Therefore they are able to maintain their mental balance avoiding excessive joy or grief.

Another couplet indicates how the wise people steer their lives in the society.

Wisdom is to love in tune with the mode
of the changing world.

Kural 426

Society is moving according to times. What was good yesterday may not be good today. What was justice some years back may be injustice today. The wise people understand the above concept. They move with the changing face of the society and are accepted by society. This is called worldly wisdom or common sense. Another important lesson in improving social relations is seeking the blessings and guidance of great people by befriending them.

Value merit of men with morals and sagacity
and secure their amity.

Kural 441

Centuries ago our kings and monarchs worshipped sages and monks and accepted them as their Gurus, friends, philosophers and guides.

For common people like us there are a number of wise virtuous people who can guide us. Respecting them and accepting their guidance will help us always.

Ten times worse is to lose good friends
than to face countless foes.

Kural 450

Good friends will come to your help when you are in trouble. Such being the case giving up good friendship is really bad. This couplet stresses giving up friendship is worse than being hated by foe.

'Tell me about your friends. I will tell you who you are' is an adage. Society assesses you after seeing you through your friends. Hence it is necessary to maintain friendship of good and wise people.

Thiruvalluvar advises all people to know their duty to society and carry out the same without any hesitation. One who respects the society should naturally respect all the members of the society. Doing his duty to society is in fact an exhibition of his respect to society.

Giving is a Gift of God

All riches that tireless efforts fetch
are to help those deserving much.

Kural 212

Wealth is not only money. It may be in the form of knowledge, skills or capacity to do hard work. They are of any value only if they are utilised to help those in society who deserve the same.

A few more couplets reiterate the same idea with some striking examples.

Duty expects not anything in return
just as rain expects none.

Kural 211

One who discharges duty to the society should not expect anything back from the society. The rain helps us in a number of ways. But there is no way by which we can recompense its help except by helping others in our own way.

The wealth of the truly wise is like
the brimming village tank.

Kural 215

Water in a drinking water pond is used by all the members of the society without any discrimination. In the same manner the wealth earned by the wise and kind-hearted people will be useful to a number of deserving people without any discrimination of caste, creed etc.

Wealth of a generous man is like a herbal tree
that becomes an unfailing remedy.

Kural 217

A herbal tree in a habitat is useful to all. The curing effects of its various parts are made use of by one and all to cure their diseases. Similarly the wealth of a broad-minded person will be useful to one and all in the society.

In this chapter we have quoted a number of couplets from *Thirukkural* exalting a number of virtues. If people take it upon themselves to cultivate these virtues and maintain them, the society in which they live will definitely be a beautiful place. A number of simple qualities have been advocated by Thiruvalluvar. A smiling face, using kind words, controlling anger, pleasing manners and avoiding slander are definitely some good qualities which one can cultivate with little extra efforts. These qualities help improve our relations with fellow human beings, ultimately our harmonious social relations improve our quality of life. They also help improve corporate relationships.

Public Relations

MODERN MANAGEMENT concepts centre around maintenance of good human relations. The manager has to trust his own people. He should believe that his workers are willing to work. Workers are the greatest assets of an organisation, compared to other movable or immovable properties shown in the balance sheets. The manager should understand that self-respect of his workers should be boosted in order to increase the productivity and achieve the objective of the industry. Workers should be encouraged to take part in managing the affairs of the industry to the extent possible. The management should be tolerant with minor mistakes of the workers and understand that 'without mistakes there can be no progress'. Management should take care to maintain good industrial relations and develop the workers. On maintenance of proper human relations, *Thirukkural* has a lot to convey.

Love begets the life of love for others
and amity of excellence it yields.

Kural 74

Love and affection shown by the manager to his subordinates yield aspiration. This love also inspires them and enkindles the feeling of friendship. When the feeling of friendship is around, it ensures high level of cooperation, which ultimately leads to carrying out programmes as per schedule in order to achieve the company's objectives. Hence, love and affection are the first positive steps in human relations.

Kind words with a smiling face
are better than gifts of grace.

Kural 92

We know that to give is a virtuous act. If it is given wholeheartedly, it is a great virtue. *Thirukkural* points out that sweet words from smiling face are still greater and carry more value than whole-hearted giving. As such managers stand to benefit by using sweet words as they go a long way in maintaining cordial human relations.

Humility and sweet words are one's jewels.
All others are not at all jewels.

Kural 95

In this kural, Thiruvalluvar goes one step further in improving human relations. Apart from speaking sweet words, he expects one to be humble. If one is humble when his position is high he is looked upon with respect. These qualities help him to improve human relations all around.

Forgetting the good is no good but it's good
to forget at once what is not good.

Kural 108

It is an essential lesson in human relations. If somebody does some good, it is necessary to bear it in mind. On the other hand, it is equally necessary to forget any wrong done to you. 'Forgive and forget' is the saying to remember. This attitude will not only give you mental peace but also go a long way in improving human relations.

Not being one-sided like an even balance
is an ornament to the wise.

Kural 118

A manager should always be neutral in his dealings. Whether it is for finding the competence of his subordinates or assessing the tenders of various suppliers for making purchase orders, sale orders or contracts, a manager should be neutral. He should not show undue bias either towards or against any person. He should act like a balance and deal, keeping merits in view. This quality will not only add fame to him but also develop the interests of his organisation.

Tending others' goods as his own
is a merchant's best transaction.

Kural 120

It is the duty of the manager to see that his business prospers. We are in the world of consumers. Their interests are to be protected. As such, a trader's interest very much depends on consumer's satisfaction. Hence, in order to serve the interest of his own business, a manager has to take care of the service rendered by his organisation to others. This is a good lesson in consumer relations.

Control your tongue if not anything; otherwise
a slip of the tongue brings evils.

Kural 127

This advice is apt for all human beings. However, all the more it applies to a manager. If he wants to maintain good interpersonal relations, it is necessary for a manager to guard his tongue. Any foul word coming out of his mouth may spoil the best of relations maintained for years together. It may spoil the interest of the organisation and the personal interest of the manager himself in the long run. Hence, it is necessary on the part of the manager to check and avoid words which may bring discredit or which are likely to be misinterpreted.

Who cannot live in harmony with the world
though learned, are fools indeed.

Kural 140

This is a very good advice for the present-day managers. They might have learnt a lot in every field of management but unless they know and understand the people around them and the people with whom they are working, they will not be in a position to apply even a fraction of what they have learnt. Thiruvalluvar has given paramount importance to human relations as a tool of management in order to make the management techniques more effective.

Though others do intolerable harm, pity them
and better it is to do no evil to them.

Kural 157

This is not only a lesson for developing one into a perfect manager but also a perfect human being. A manager should not think about 'tit for tat' either with his subordinates or colleagues. Such a method will create a chain reaction and take the overall situation to a bad state of human relations, which may not be conducive even for maintaining status quo, let alone development.

Evil is feared more than fire
as evil begets evil ever.

Kural 202

A manager should shun evil. He should restrain himself from doing things which are evil in nature, because bad things will result only in worst consequence which may spoil human relations and shake the confidence of all those working together towards common goal. Just like fire destroys everything, evil also spoils the entire surroundings. As such, an able manager shuns from doing anything bad to those around him.

If everyone sees his faults as he sees others'
will any evil ever fall on living beings?

Kural 190

Every man should have a method of dealing with his own defects so as to rectify them. Instead of finding fault with others if a manager views his workers' lapses from another angle and sees what he should have done to prevent the same, it would be easy for him to check such failures in future and come out successful. This is an aspect of positive thinking to be appreciated and developed by modern managers to improve their respective fields.

'What is truth?' if the question be
it's speech with words evil-free.

Kural 291

This is an apt definition of truth to be understood and learnt by all modern managers. If a manager has access to confidential information, he should not divulge them as it may bring him as also others irreparable harm. Under such circumstances, it is better not to divulge fact, unless it becomes absolutely unavoidable. Definition of truth here is what will not bring harm.

If a manager adopts such an attitude, he can save others with grace, which will go a long way in maintaining good human relations.

Even untruth has the stamp of truthfulness
if it brings good sans harmfulness.

Kural 292

This couplet of *Thirukkural* gives one more dimension to the concept of truth. We generally consider truth as a statement of fact. It may be generally so. But on some other occasions, it may be different. If an untruth brings good in the end by removing evil, it can also be considered as truth. After all, is it not our objective to eradicate evil and establish good?

In fact, this is a step ahead on the previous couplet, one desists from speaking truth if it brings harm. As per this couplet, one speaks even false if it brings good.

Envy, the matchless sinner, ruins wealth
and directs her sister to the envious.

Kural 168

In order to maintain the best of human relations, one has to give up the evil called envy or jealousy that spoils a man from within and makes everybody else hate him. If a manager nurtures this emotion, it will not be possible for him to better his relations with those around him. Therefore, it is crystal clear that if one shuns jealousy and envy, he will do an excellent job in improving human relations.

The above couplet is not only for the saints who want salvation but applies to any living human being. It can also apply for managers. Compassion is the quality which makes a manager outstanding in a company and makes others respect him. The respect and regard that compassion brings make him improve relations for the betterment of the organisation.

Fire of anger that guts all who draw near it
burns kinship, the life-boat.

Kural 306

It is a very apt lesson for all practicing managers. They should avoid anger at any cost. Anger is the worst of all negative feelings. Thiruvalluvar has correctly described anger as something which kills those whom it touches. How? It spoils all the hard earned friendship and kinship. How can a man or for that matter a manager maintain good human relations if friendship and kinship are lost. Anger is one quality which when a manager loses, he gains in terms of better relations.

Sorrows are not for those with merciful heart.
This wind-blown world bears witness to it.

Kural 245

Compassion or mercy is a positive feeling which lifts up the spirit of a manager. It kindles positive feeling among those around him, helping him maintain proper and balanced human relations.

Humility alone is the might of the mighty.
It's a weapon to transform enmity.

Kural 985

Humility is a very effective instrument in the hands of a manager. Whatever may be his capacity and competence, with one good quality called humility, he can even transform the minds of his bosses and make them his friends. Then, he can easily achieve his objectives.

All these couplets show us the path to develop and maintain proper human relations. Proper human relations help a manager understand his team-mates in proper perspective. It also helps other team members understand him better. It is this understanding which brings about proper coordination and makes them work together towards common objectives. The human resource of a company is more important than everything. Hence, they have to be treated with respect.

Moreover, self-respect should not be hurt. It has to be recognised and honoured. Only then the efficiency and productivity of the organisation will improve. People who are respected and loved develop to the utmost. They try to learn more and gain knowledge. Their competence improves and they become self-disciplined. There is no necessity to enforce discipline by adopting tough measures, as they are already self-disciplined.

When people take initiative and carry out their jobs effectively, there is no necessity for close supervision. By improving human relations and maintaining the same at an optimum level, a manager can 'manage' effectively.

எண்ணித் துணிக கருமந் துணிந்தபின்
எண்ணுவ மென்ப திழுக்கு

தூங்குக தூங்கிச் செயற்பால தூங்கற்க
தூங்காது செய்யும் வினை

Communication Skills

ONE OF the greatest challenges of the present day executives is to communicate effectively. Be it to customers, peers, employees, or the boss, the executive has to talk without offence.

What is true of day to day life applies equally to the corporate world. It is words, not just knowledge and education that make or mar one's success. This is more ironical, since one of the greatest preoccupations of humanity—apart from eating, sleeping and fighting—has been 'talking'. Pardon those who do extra-shifts of the important work even in sleeping! While many talk their way to success, there are some who will draw themselves with this obsession.

The subject of 'Communication' has always been the pet topic for many management experts. A few could probably even manage multiple doctorates for this. Like a Hindu God, this subject has taken many manifestations. As for future Avatars in store, may be, God only knows. Communication skills are very much necessary for a manager to be successful in his endeavours. Communication means to make the listener understand things as the communicator would like to understand him. Let us see what Thiruvalluvar has to say in respect of communication skills. Why should a manager or for that matter any human being need such skills?

Words are the Ambassadors of Ideas

The world will always be quick to execute
the words that are sweetly well-set.

Kural 648

A manager is a leader of a team. The team has to listen to him and carry out his various instructions in letter and spirit in order to achieve the company's objectives. In order to achieve the same, it is essential for a good manager to be an astute communicator.

An astute communicator spells out his ideas in eloquent and sweet language so that his ideas reach the persons at the other end. It should be so, irrespective of the fact that the other person is his boss, subordinate, colleague or society at large. When his ideas reach the other persons they carry out his suggestions, requests or instructions as the case may be. As such, we can see in the words of Thiruvalluvar that it is essential that a good manager should be an astute communicator.

Communication culminates in Constructive Execution

One can never be an efficient executive without a command over verbal communication. The main task of an executive is to get things done which starts with speaking to others. So, good communication is an essential and primary qualification. It is also something more and different from other faculties of an executive. Thiruvalluvar says that an executive who possesses this in abundance can even conquer the world.

Gain or loss depends on one's words.
So guard against slip in words.

Kural 642

How does one becomes an astute communicator? Here also *Thirukkural* is able to guide the manager.

Language apt for Listeners

Those with pure mind and studied eloquence
should use words that suit the audience.

Kural 711

When a manager communicates he should first of all think about the audience with whom he is going to communicate. Only if what he talks and how he talks suits his audience they will be able to understand him.

Conceive Communication in Mind

By virtue of his position, the executive enjoys certain powers. So his words, right or wrong, become the law. If he does not guard his tongue, damage may be irreparable and irreversible. After all, others cannot penetrate into the speaker's mind and find out what exactly he thinks or wants to say. When the message is loud, it is taken to be clear and correct. The executive should appreciate that a word out of the mouth whether intentional or otherwise, is like an arrow out of the bow. Even if it is nothing but accidental firing, it is bound to hit.

Code of spotless men is to say what is desirable
and grasp from others what is useful.

Kural 646

Essential Ingredients

A speech should have the ingredients of flawlessness, brevity, clarity, sweetness and purpose. To get to the basics, when there is a talk, there can be only two types of audiences: one set of people, who are hearing and the other who are not. Naturally, a good speech is one that the audience wants to hear for more time and others, who are not hearing now, are also encouraged to hear.

Be it a board meeting, with the chairperson's speech or a parliamentary debate on a vital subject or quite simply a farewell address, all of us have experienced unadulterated boredom. On the other hand, there are veterans who can steal the show with just a vote of thanks to deliver. Thus the side dish at times is more delicious than the main course, because the person delivering the same has not only taken care of the above ingredients but has also mastered the art of blending them in the right proportion.

Imagine this experience we have in a buffet lunch at a five-star hotel: First, from a distance, all the items look attractive; then as we go near, the flavour and aroma activate our nostrils; then the feel (sponginess or crispness) of the items; then comes the real taste, not to forget the after effects. This is true of a good speech or any communication, circular, notices, advertisements, etc.

The gift of the gab is the best of gifts
and forms not part of other gifts.

Kural 641

Sweet Words

Only if the language, words and tone are adopted in such a way that the audience is attracted by his speech and understand them, the speaker will be able to transfer his ideas across the minds of the audience. That is what exactly is the objective of proper communication. It is the shared purpose of a shared understanding.

Let us learn more in this regard from Thiruvalluvar.

Always utter fruitful words.
Never utter futile words.

Kural 200

This couplet teaches the art of communication to a manager. If what a manager intends to tell somebody is not effective and of no use, then it is better that he refrains from such communication. On the other hand, if what he proposes to tell others is effective and useful he should definitely speak out. Also, while communicating with others one should use only the barest minimum words which are essential for communication and avoid all sorts of unnecessary words which are described as useless by Thiruvalluvar.

Communicator vs Listener

Next come the main aspects of communication viz. speaking and listening. The test of good eloquence is that it should be desired by the listener. The problem does not end here. It is necessary that a good communicator should also be able to understand the substance of the words spoken by others. We can easily see the dual duties of effective communication. The golden rule is, 'When you speak, be sure, others like to hear you. But when you are a listener, your efforts should be to understand properly what is being told'. Oh! How often we reverse the roles!

An efficient, tireless and fearless speaker
is hard for anyone to conquer.

Kural 647

It is generally observed that there are two common bottlenecks to success viz. fear and lack of perseverance. The kural guarantees that the person who has mastered the art of speech will be fearless and indefatigable. To win over him is, hence pretty difficult.

What is needed of an executive is the art of effectively putting across his thoughts in tune with the listener. In real-life situations, be it office or any other place, we come across people who are confident and unassailable. Such people are those who are articulate who have mastered the skill of speech. World over, politicians will stand testimony to this.

The world will always be quick to execute
the words that are sweetly well set.

Kural 648

What every executive essentially hopes is that the work prescribed by him should be carried out. Here is a simple solution suggested. Valluvar observes that, even the whole world, will carry out the executive's orders provided, the instructions are placed in proper order and told pleasantly. *Thirukkural* couplets themselves are standing examples for this. He restricts all his good ideas to two lines. A good manager can follow his example by expressing himself in brief.

Communication—Two-way Process

Whoever can read another's unspoken mind
is a jewel of the sea-locked world.

Kural 701

Most of us think communication is a one-sided affair in which the manager would just speak out what he wants to communicate. Communication, however, has got two sides, one being the speaker's side and the other the listener's side. Unless the listener (audience) hears and understands what one speaks there is no use in speaking. How the listener receives one's speech should be taken note of by the speaker if he wants to be an astute communicator. A listener makes himself understood by his facial expressions and gestures or body languages. A good manager should be able to understand the body language of others and grasp what is in their minds. If he can do that his communication will be a real success and he will be a real success and will be an asset to his organisation.

Let us go to another couplet which stresses the importance of the art of listening.

Listening is the wealth of wealth.
It is the crown of all wealth.

Kural 411

Unless a manager listens to his workers or his team-mates it will not be possible for him to get proper feedback. The essence of communication lies in feedback and unless the manager knows whether his team-mates have understood his instructions and they will carry them out as per the programme he cannot rest assured of the results. He cannot plan further.

Under the above circumstances, the art of listening gains importance. Whether it is listening to the words or the body language it is a great asset, says Thiruvalluvar.

A Slip of Tongue Snaps the Deal

The art of communication is hailed by Thiruvalluvar as a powerful tool. Various couplets on the title, 'Power of Speech' explain the same unequivocally. Thiruvalluvar warns us of slip of the tongue.

Control your tongue if not anything; otherwise
a slip of the tongue brings evils.

Kural 127

We already saw in a previous couplet that proper words and, intonation make a speech successful and make people carry out the commands, suggestions or requests as the case may be. On the other hand, any slip of tongue can lead only to ruin. As such, we should guard ourselves from any slip of the tongue whenever we are speaking.

Let Audience be Addressed

What holds the audience spellbound and reach
others and make them long for, is a speech.

Kural 643

A good communication is one that binds the men to whom it is spoken by the speaker. A manager should learn that sort of communication. Speech should be such that even those who did not hear the speech and those who are averse to such speeches will be interested to hear the same after hearing. The importance of powerful communication is reiterated in subsequent *Thirukkural* couplets also.

Weigh and utter your words very well
that no virtue and wealth can excel.

Kural 644

Words are more powerful than virtue or wealth, if properly chosen and properly spoken.

This is a lesson this couplet teaches us. Should we not be very careful when words are so powerful? Cannot we achieve our objective, if we choose speech as a powerful tool?

Who cannot express their love to others
are like a bunch of scentless flowers.

Kural 650

An astute communicator should be able to express himself clearly. He should properly explain what he has learnt whenever required. Unless he expresses himself powerfully, what he has learnt may not be of any use. His learning will be compared to flowers without fragrance. Hence, it is necessary on the part of a manager to learn the art of communication so that whatever he has learnt is made use of.

Code of spotless men is to say what is desirable
and grasp from others what is useful.

Kural 646

This *Thirukkural* couplet reiterates once again both sides of communication. When one is speaking and another is listening, one should speak in a desirable manner so that those at the other end are attracted by it. On the other hand, whatever others talk, whether it is sweet, sour or somewhat unintelligible, one should be able to grasp the main points from it. Only then will the art of communication be complete. Otherwise, it will only be half accomplished.

Communication Conquers.

Finally, Thiruvalluvar describes an astute communicator as below.

An efficient, tireless and fearless speaker
is hard for anyone to conquer.

Kural 647

The essential attributes of a powerful communicator have been expressed in this verse. He should be flawless in his speech. He should not have any fear of the audience. He should use all the power at his command without exhaustion. If he has these qualities nobody can defeat him. As such, we can see that an astute communicator becomes a very successful person.

After learning about the importance of communication, a manager should utilise it as an effective tool in achieving the objectives of his organisation.

Any communication generally makes some demands on the listeners. It may be with an intention of conveying some orders or some proposals. It is a tool by which the desired changes are brought about. Otherwise, failure of communication will result in utter chaos. To avoid such failure, listening and understanding are very important.

The use of language and words should be such that everyone understands what is being conveyed. Whether the points have been well understood should also be checked in all-important cases by proper feedback. Feedback shows whether the communication has the desired results. Under the above circumstances communication failure can be avoided. A communication is said to be complete only when it is acknowledged.

In other words, what is said and how it is said is based upon how it is heard and understood. Only when both the processes are in synchronised communication can there be success. This is what has been reiterated in various *Thirukkural* couplets, explained in this chapter.

Thus, the art of communication is an effective tool in the hands of a good manager.

Human Resources Management

HUMAN RESOURCE Management is one of the most important branches of management because it is the human factor which finally decides the success or failure of an organisation. The branch of management which deals with the human factor is called Human Resource Management. Human Resource management deals with many different aspects of the organisational structure. Recruitment, supervision, training and development, promotion, disciplinary action, welfare and industrial relations are the main categories coming under Human Resource Management. Let us see what *Thirukkural* has to say on Human Resource Management.

Education vs Knowledge

Even great scholars free from vice
are seldom free from ignorance.

Kural 503

Generally when employees are recruited for an organisation, some minimum educational qualifications are prescribed.

It may be necessary because that is how one can limit the number of eligible applicants. But on the other hand, just because somebody has the necessary educational qualification one cannot simply select him. Whether he has the knowledge necessary for that job has to be tested. This *Thirukkural* couplet tells us that even highly educated people are not free from ignorance. As such, their knowledge in that particular field has to be specially tested if they are to be employed. A job for a man and a man for a job.

Experience is Essential

For the greatness or the meanness of men
their deeds are the touchstone.

Kural 505

When a job needs prior experience we cannot simply recruit freshers for that job. We have to choose men with proper and adequate experience. His performance will be the criterion for selection. His past performance and past achievements should be taken into consideration. The selection should be based on performance. That alone should guide the personnel manager in coming to proper conclusion.
Another couplet indicates the folly of improper selection.

Nepotism negates the Objectives

Choosing persons of incompetence
out of love brings all ignorance.

Kural 507

In selection favouritism and nepotism should be avoided at any cost. This point is well brought out in this *Thirukkural* couplet. If under any circumstances or under some pressure one chooses a person who is ignorant of the job and who is not suitable in any manner, it can only lead to the creation of problems in the company or office. Thiruvalluvar has most vocally stated that what will ensue is folly in all its forms.

We may take this *Thirukkural* couplet as a continuation to the previous couplet. After entrusting the responsibilities, it is also the duty of the manager to help the worker put in his best. Whatever facilities he needs should be provided to him so that he can do his best.

Trust is the Touchstone

Trusting sans testing and doubting the tested
will lead to great woes without end.

Kural 510

As explained in detail in a number of previous couplets, a manager has to trust a person only after assessing his suitability. Once the assessment is over and the job is entrusted to the individual, we should not go on doubting him every now and then. If we entrust the job without proper test, and if we go on doubting after entrusting the job to an individual it will only create trouble for us. Hence, we should avoid both.

Fortune forsakes one who disbelieves
loyalty of diligent workers.

Kural 519

If somebody is doing his duty with devotion and dedication, we should permit him to complete his job. If we go on doubting him, it may not yield good results. It will lead us only to ruin. All managers should take care to encourage duty-conscious people in the interest of the organisation.

Eternal Vigilance eliminates Inefficiency

Nowadays, vigilance wings have come to stay as part of Human Resource Management in various organisations. *Thirukkural* tells us even about these vigilance organisations and how to run them.

King's duty is to learn from spies promptly
all happenings to his subjects daily.

Kural 582

A manager should know what is happening in his organisation. Otherwise, he cannot take timely corrective measures. In order to set things right at the appropriate time, he should know what is going on and happening to everybody at all times in his organisation.

Thirukkural guides us about how to keep track of everything happening in the company.

A spy is the one who spies on king's officials,
his own relatives and enemies.

Kural 584

The vigilance wing should take care of all these duties. Those who are involved in various types of work, those who are close to the manager and those who are against him should be watched keenly by the working spies. They will report about the various activities carried out by those workers. How can these worthy spies gather intelligence?

Unsuspected appearance, roving eyes
and keeping secrets mark the spies.

Kural 585

They should view things and persons without any fear or favour. They should try to gather information in any guise they deem fit. They should be able to guard all secrets without revealing them to others either knowingly or unknowingly. These are all the various qualities expected of a worthy spy.

A spy is one who searches other's secrets out
and confirms them beyond doubt.

Kural 587

A spy who gathers information should not be satisfied with mere rumours and pass it on to his boss. He should verify whatever he gathers and clear it beyond doubt. Only after confirming the fact, he should pass it on to his boss for further action. Or else, only chaos will result in the organisation.

How to act on intelligence so gathered depends on the importance of the matter.

Confirm not merely on one spy's report
but verify it with another's report.

Kural 588

If the matter is very important and if any action taken (based on the intelligence report) is likely to have long-ranging effects, then it is better to verify the intelligence report through some other source before taking action. This is a very important advice given by Thiruvalluvar to all practicing managers.

Redressal of Grievances advances Promotion

A Human Resource Manager is generally in charge of the administration of an organisation. As such, he has to redress the grievances of the employees and take care of their welfare. In case the organisation is 'dealing with redressal of public grievances or consumer's grievances, these matters will be looked after by the manager concerned.'

Thirukkural guides the Human Resource Manager regarding rules he should follow in running the administration in a proper as well as innovative fashion so as to bring the desired results. Those couplets are discussed in detail in the ensuing paragraphs.

As the whole world looks to the sky for rainfall,
all subjects look to the king for just rule.

Kural 542

What has been mentioned as a king's role applies now to the manager in the modern world. All the employees of the organisation look for justice to be rendered by the Human Resource Manager, just like the earth looks up to the sky for rains. As such, a personnel manager has to take upon himself the duty to render justice without any deviation and in a transparent manner. Not only that justice should be done but also it should be evident that it has been done.

The inaccessible and unrighteous chief
perishes in disgraceful grief.

Kural 548

When some employee approaches the individual with a grievance, the manager should be accessible. He should be available to the employees. He should also appear simple and humble so that the employees can make their representation without any hesitation whatsoever. Then only the employees will have the confidence that the manager will listen to them. If the manager is inaccessible or he takes a defiant attitude, that will bring ruin not only to himself but also to the whole organisation.

None is Unequal

Not lance but scepter swayed with equity
alone gives the king victory.

Kural 546

This *Thirukkural* couplet illustrates that positive reinforcement is the method which brings success, rather than negative reinforcement. If a manager is straightforward in his dealings, it earns him due regard among his employees and colleagues and brings him success in all his endeavours.

Gracefulness Gains

The whole world surely belongs to those
who are benign and aware of duties.

Kural 578

A Human Resource Manager has to be gracious in his outlook. At the same time, he should be dutiful. His gracious outlook should not stop him from discharging his duties impartially.

Such a man who can be gracious on one hand and who can discharge his duties effectively on the other has a right to head his organisation. Personnel management has a role to play in respect of discipline of the employees. *Thirukkural* has a lot to say in this respect.

Enquiring, favouring no one, being impartial,
consulting and rendering justice is just rule.

Kural 541

While taking disciplinary action and awarding punishment, a manager has to act impartially. He should not be selective in taking action. The laws should be interpreted and applied to all in a just and fair manner after proper consultation, if necessary.

Be Impartial, Weed Out Inefficiency

Unkind speech and excessive penalties
Erode king's winning power like files.

Kural 567

A manager should take enough care to see that he does not use rough and rude language when talking to his employees. It always pays to be polite. Also, while awarding punishments, he should take care that the punishments are proportionate to the gravity of the misconduct. The punishment should not be unduly harsh. Otherwise, his authority and power will not be given regard.

Lift the rod firmly but strike very gently.
It ensures long stay of prosperity.

Kural 562

A manager should also be an actor. It may be necessary for him to put on a show at times. This can be termed as 'diplomatic' management.

Before erring employees, a manager should put up a show as if he is going to be very strict. However, while awarding punishment he has to be reasonable. This diplomacy is required on the part of a manager to maintain proper discipline and at the same time to ensure that his employees are not unduly hurt.

Passing death sentence on cruel murderers
is like removing weeds from green fields.

Kural 550

The manager has got every justification to punish the bad. That point is stressed in this *Thirukkural* couplet. Even though a manager is expected to be careful, reasonable and diplomatic in taking disciplinary action and awarding punishment, he should not shove his responsibility in this regard. Punishing those involved in severe misdeeds and crimes are equivalent to removal of weed from a crop field. Only if the weeds are removed will the crops survive. Is it not the duty of the farmers to save the crops? Similarly, it becomes the duty of the manager to ensure the growth of the organisation by removing miscreants. The manager should not have any hesitation whatsoever in performing that duty. Those are all the things a manager should know regarding discipline in administration.

Efficiency vs Effectiveness

Another aspect of HR Management is training and development. Thiruvalluvar has written a few couplets regarding this also, though rather indirectly.

Learn well whatever is worthy of learning.
Then act according to that learning.

Kural 391

When an employee undergoes training he should learn thoroughly all the aspects which are taught to him without leaving out anything. However, after the training is over, he should not forget or ignore what he has learnt. He should remember them and put them into practice. That is the essential idea of training. This is something which the management should not forget.

Learning is supreme imperishable wealth.
Other things are not real wealth.

Kural 400

If an employee learns the techniques of his job through proper training, it is a great asset to him. It is not only an asset to the individual but to the organisation as well.

Listening is the wealth of wealth.
It is the crown of all wealth.

Kural 411

Here we understand that listening refers to proper training. Proper training is considered to be the greatest of all wealth. Listening during training not only improves the knowledge of the employee but also improves his techniques and hand-on experience. As such, it is termed as the greatest of wealth.

Even if the wise understand incorrectly,
they never speak foolishly.

Kural 417

During proper training, an employee who listens well and learns sharply is benefited very much. By such foolproof training, he will never speak or act foolishly even by slip of the tongue. As such, his performance will be excellent and will also improve the performance of the organisation.

Weigh the act, your own might, foes' might
and allies' might and proceed straight

kural 471

Another not so uncommon mistake managers tend to make is to underestimate the opponent's strength. Before waging a war, the opponent's capabilities are to be kept in mind. Otherwise, the effect would be that of placing the opponent in conditions where his growth is assured. History has such innumerable examples, like Alexander the Great. Similarly, a hasty act on the part of the manager, without weighing the strengths and strategies of those opposing him, will only nurture their growth. This is true of launching a product or handling a trade union issue.

Deliberate and do what the world will approve.
Or else your act the world won't approve.

Kural 470

When there is an urge to complete the task, there is generally a temptation to follow any means. The king and his planners should be careful to adopt such means and methodologies, which are consistent and commensurate with one's own capabilities. In managerial parlance, we may say that, the manager shall keep in view his own status and strength.

Project Management

PROJECT MANAGEMENT has been dealt with in detail, straight from conception to completion, in many couplets. Modern concepts of project management find their origin in *Thirukkural* couplets. Let us deal with these couplets in detail. The first couplet we are going to examine gives us an idea of how a project has to be conceived.

Conception of a Project

Resources, means, time, place and deed.
Examine these five before you proceed.

Kural 675

The various aspects which have to be dealt with before selecting a project are outlined here. Firstly, the project which is proposed to be taken up has to be decided. This can be decided, depending on various options available.

Finance

Finance is the first and foremost necessity for carrying out any scheme as and when it is selected. The source of finance, the rate of interest and the method of repayment etc, should be given due consideration. The viability of the scheme should also be checked. Before pumping in much money into the project, one should consider to question whether the returns will be sufficient for the repayment of loans and whether there will be money left out for dividends and future expansions or not.

The Three Ms

The means of carrying out the work also deserves due consideration. It should be checked whether the organisation has adequate men and materials to carry out the scheme. If not, the work has to be given on contract. All these things should be done, based on certain decided norms.

Time Managment

Time is also a criterion in projects. When the work should commence and within what period it should be completed should also be well thought out and decided, depending on requirements.

The whole world is his who acts
at the right time and place.

Kural 484

A Project Manager should bear it in mind that his project has to be completed within a fixed gestation period. Various activities of the project should be completed in the time slots allotted. If we choose the time and place, to suit the nature of activity, we can even conquer the world.

When rare and ripe opportunity arrives
venture at once into rare deeds.

Kural 489

Carrying out the activities at appropriate time is stressed in this *Thirukkural* couplet. 'Time and tide wait for no man', says the proverb. As such, we should not hesitate to carry out the job when time is ripe. If we hesitate we may have to wait for the next season and the project may get prolonged. However tough our assignment may be, if a manager plans it in the appropriate time, he can succeed with ease.

Location

The place in which the work should be carried out is also a matter of great importance. It has to be decided, taking various factors relevant to the project into consideration.

As we discussed initially, the nature of the project has to be decided first. Based on the same, a feasibility report has to be chalked out. Thus, activity, place, time, money and means have to be considered in detail before launching a project.

Collection of Resources

When an electrical undertaking wants to generate more

power to meet growing demands, it decides to go in for installing a new coal based thermal station. First of all, it should be near a mine or coal has to be transported. As transport cost has to be minimum, it has to be erected near a seaport. With it, raw water and cooling water problems should also be solved.

Competent Men to Handle

The work has to be carried out by contract by competent companies, decided by open tender. Based on the demand projection and power requirement, the date on which the project should commence and the date on which it should go on stream are decided. All these aspects should be covered in the feasibility report. Regarding finance, one has to decide on the source of finance. The quantum of money and when and how they will be made available and repayment schedules are also to be taken care of in these proposals.

In the couplet above we saw that a project has to be selected first. How to select the activity? Here also *Thirukkural* helps us.

Weigh the Pros and Cons

Judge the mode of completion, hurdles and gain
before you plunge into an action.

Kural 676

When we select a project the following things are to be taken into consideration. The efforts which are to be undertaken for completion of a project, various factors which may hinder the execution of the project straight from conception and the profits, which we may gain on completion of projects, are the criteria to be taken into consideration before deciding upon the project.

Execution by Experts

After beginning a project, following steps have to be taken.

Learning the tactics from an expert
is the best way to do an act.

Kural 677

The policy of appointing experts as consultants has come to stay. But the above policy was emphasised by Thiruvalluvar two thousand years ago. If a scheme has to be completed successfully within a time-frame, physical and financial targets are to be coordinated and if the results are to be fruitful, then it is necessary that experts who have sufficient experience and knowledge are consulted before taking up the work.

Doing one deed by another deed similar
is like luring one tusker by another.

Kural 678

When we take up a project, we may have one objective in mind. However, when we study the feasibility and work out the details with some effort, we can achieve another objective as well. If that is possible we can take up the work.

When sugar factories are established bagasse is the effluent that is left behind. It takes a lot of money and effort if the effluent is to be disposed. On the other hand, a cogeneration plant can be established and the bagasse utilised effectively to generate power. The power so generated can be used not only for manufacture of sugar but also surplus can be sold to the state grid. This is a solid example of achieving another useful activity by the deed originally proposed. As such, when we take up a project, even though single-minded devotion is absolutely necessary for completing it, an one-track mind should be avoided. If we can carry out any other gainful economic activity by some little extra effort and if it is beneficial in the long run, we might as well plan for it simultaneously and carry it out too.

Preparatory Work shall Precede

Better do deeds whenever feasible, or else
act after finding proper time and place.

Kural 673

A project comprises various activities. Certain activities can be taken up only on completion of previous activities. They are serial activities. Certain other activities can be taken up simultaneously as parallel activities.

Hence, these activities are carried out simultaneously without waiting. However, serial activities are taken up only on completion of the previous activities, ie. as and when feasible. Taking up the completion of works will be as per

PERT chart, comprising all activities from beginning to the end as prepared by the engineers.

Delay Breeds Corruption

Delay only the deeds that merit delay.
Delay not deeds that merit no delay.

Kural 672

These are the lessons to be learnt from this *Thirukkural* couplet. A manager need not carry out all acts with the same speed. There are certain works which can be delayed. Some other works which are not of immediate relevance and which will not result in cost escalation if done slowly can be delayed by giving preference to more important jobs. However, the work which will lead to cost escalation should be carried out without undue delay.

This *Thirukkural* couplet also makes us realise the relevance of the PERT chart. Serial activities can be carried out only one after the other. For instance, if a machine has to be erected on a plinth, the plinth has to be constructed first. Only after the plinth is completed the machine can be erected. At the same time, when the plinth is constructed, simultaneously the machine can be assembled to the extent it can be erected safely on the plinth. That is when the construction of plinth and erection of machine are serial activities. Plinth construction and assembling of machine are parallel activities. Hence, we can understand that when a subsequent serial activity has to be delayed, a parallel activity should be carried out without any undue delay.

Waver not on acts resolved but act firmly,
fearlessly and wakefully.

Kural 668

We learnt from the previous couplet that certain activities have to be carried out without any undue delay. The same point is stressed in this couplet. Once we decide to take up a particular work at a particular moment, we should not waver. We should commence the said job without any hesitation. We should not feel tired either mentally or physically. On the other hand, we should be quick and alive to the situation and see that the work is completed as resolved for a particular purpose with single-minded devotion so that the activity is completed on time.

SWOT: A Condition Precedent

Strength, Weakness, Opportunity, and Threat from opponents shall be carefully analysed while taking important decisions in work place. It is difficult to quantify the strength of the task or the opponent, but all the same, the executive has a mental picture, an estimate of the relative strengths. As far as the task is concerned, how controversial the decision is not indicated in its strength. As for the executive embarking on the task, the strength, would mean and include his own stature in the organisation, his track record and his competence.

What is normally not estimated but is generally underestimated or frequently overestimated is the strength of the opponents or of the competitors. The reality is that, it is a factor to be reckoned with. In a way, it is like playing a game of chess. It will not suffice to plan one's moves. It is more important to assess the opponent's likely moves too.

In real-life situations, be it launching of a product, closing an office or transferring a person, there won't be just two opposing forces. Each side would be supported by others, whose influence and impact are also to be taken into account. As experience shows, sometimes the supporters' strength far exceeds that of the main opponent!

Any important decision such as managerial, commercial or even political has to be preceded by the above thought process and more often than not, it is actually done so.

Another point to be borne in mind by a project manager is the place. If a job is carried out in the appropriate location, he can succeed.

They require no ally but fearless might
if a right field they choose to fight.

Kural 497

Different jobs can be done in different places. There are cottage industries which can be established in houses. Certain activities involving heavy machinery are confined only to the factories. Certain other industrial activities could be carried out only in industrial estates with necessary infrastructure and with the help of other ancillary industries around.

As such, it is necessary to choose the proper location for the activity proposed, and the job should be carried out boldly to ensure success. The importance of carrying out an activity in the most appropriate place is stressed in one more *Thirukkural* couplet.

Begin not any task and despise not your enemies
till you find a right place to attack from all sides.

Kural 491

Even though the word 'foe' is used here, its meaning can be suitably altered to suit the modern industrial scenario. After all, the manager does not have any foes. He has only competitors! Before commencing any activity the location/ site should be surveyed or verified and only then the activity should be started so that it can be completed successfully within the time-frame fixed.

Outsourcing

In a project, various activities to be carried out may have to be entrusted to different contractors or sub-contractors, as the case may be. Here also various *Thirukkural* couplets are provided to guide us. Let us go to a couplet which we have already referred to in Personnel Management, which equally applies to Project Management.

Employ one who widens revenue sources,
promotes wealth and removes hurdles.

Kural 512

When choosing a contractor, his past record has to be taken into account. The contractor should be able to deliver the goods. He should be a man capable of making optimum use of the resources and preventing wastes. If these points are kept in mind, a proper man for the proper job can be selected. The same point is stressed in other couplets also.

Employ not favourites but only who knows ways
to achieve things overcoming all hurdles.

Kural 515

This is a good lesson in selection. Just because you are fond of somebody you should not select a man for the job on irrelevant and extraneous consideration.

Trust sans Distrust

Once work is delegated, one would expect the delegator to be satisfied and at peace and the delegatee to be happy and performing his work. But, human tendency being what it is, the delegator many a time starts doubting the efficiency and integrity of the delegatee. And this act gives great agony and distress not only to the delegatee but also to the delegator. This suspicion takes different forms, the simplest being 'nagging'. This may also result in another dangerous dimension. The opponents may exploit the discord and gain advantage.

The proper man or proper company should be selected by hard test. Only if we consider a company as the fittest for doing a particular work, after going through various relevant tests, should we award the company the contract.

This deed, by these means, if he can perform,
test him; if convinced, assign it to him.

Kural 517

This omnibus *Thirukkural* couplet which is apt to so many situations apply as well to selection of proper contracting companies for various activities of a project. In the previous couplet, we saw that selection should be based on proper test. Here the point which is stressed is that particular activity may need specific expertise. Therefore, the expertise required for a particular job should be studied and the company or individual who has the best expertise or talent in that field should be chosen and the job should be entrusted to him/her. This will ensure successful completion of the task within the specified period. If advices rendered in all these verses are well understood and implemented by a manager, then his/her project is bound to come out successfully.

Financial Management

THIRUKKURAL DEALS with various aspects of management. Each one is unique. Thiruvalluvar gave the most brilliant ideas on Financial Management even 2000 years before which are relevant even today and will be relevant tommorrow and forever.

No organisation can function without finance. But even with finance, no organisation can survive, if not properly managed. That is why financial management gains importance.

Expenditure within Limits

Lavish life of one who lives not within means
though grand, perishes without traces.

Kural 479

The above couplet not only applies to individuals but organisations as well. Just because the finance available is in plenty, one should not spend as one likes. Expenditure should be kept within limits. This is the first lesson in budgeting. If expenditure is incurred without any limits, it would initially appear that the organisation is financially sound. However, the financial health will later gradually thin out and vanish. As such, it is absolutely necessary that all expenditure should be properly budgeted and watched.

We might have come across several schemes where money is spent within a short period but the progress remains slow. To avoid such incidents, budget should be properly prepared and both financial and physical aspects should be simultaneously monitored.

Donate within your means and worth.
It's the way to guard your wealth.

Kural 477

This *Thirukkural* couplet again reiterates the basic principles of budgeting we discussed earlier. For every item of expenditure there is a limit. We should allocate the money according to the limit and we should give it measure after ascertaining the physical progress. Allocating the money within the limit and granting the same by properly measuring the physical progress will alone help in safeguarding the wealth of the organisation.

Inflow and Outflow

It matters not even if income is limited
as long as expenditure is restricted.

Kural 478

This couplet clearly indicates how revenue expenditure should be planned. Whatever may be the revenue, big or small, one should take care that the revenue expenditure does not exceed the income. When revenue budget is prepared, this aspect is to be taken care of. Every organisation has got its own methods of finding finance for its various projects. Where cash outgo is more than inflow, the management may have to face deficit budget with consequences of avoidable austerity. Finance is very important for any company.

Wealth, the unfailing light, speeds to every land
dispersing darkness at its Lord's command.

Kural 753

Wealth has been described as next only to light. As light goes to every land and every place, it removes the gloom. Similarly, to take up any project in any land, money is most essential. If we have necessary financial resources, we need not worry. Light spreads in any direction in any place. The spread of money is considered similar to it.

Accounted Money to be Used

The wealth earned through means fair
is a source of virtue and pleasure.

Kural 754

Whether it is an individual or an organisation, collection of revenue and mobilisation of income is necessary. But Thiruvalluvar insists that money should come only by fair means. He is totally against amassing wealth by unfair means. He also stresses that only if the income comes by fair means it will bring good virtue and also bliss.

We can also see from the present-day scenario that a number of organisations who have committed economic offences are struggling hard to keep their organisations from sinking. Besides, the individuals who are responsible are facing various charges are under trial. The organisations, which once earned name and fame, are not able to maintain their name. As such, we may clearly say the flourishing of business or mobilisation of income should come only by fair means, if we are to thrive in the long run.

Wise Investment

Men of wisdom won't embark on anything
and lose their capital to gain something.

Kural 463

A manager should be prudent enough to see that the money of the organisation is invested in schemes or projects which are sound. Just because the immediate gains are attractive, one should not indulge in a project in which the entire capital could be lost. The feasibility of any scheme should be analysed in depth and a correct decision should be taken. Various dimensions of financial management are clearly indicated in the single couplet below:

Acquiring, gaining, saving and sharing treasure.
Efficiency in these marks an able ruler.

Kural 385

Even though the function of a king as financial manager is defined, this applies to all financial managers who act as kings or ministers in their own organisations.

A financial manager should be able to identify various sources from which revenue or income is realised. For that, he can even discover new sources. He should also be able to collect maximum revenue from the already existing sources, of course by fair means. The money so collected should be guarded properly and protected well from loss or theft. As told in the previous couplet, we should avoid investing the same in unreliable companies. Moreover, when we take up any projects or schemes, adequate precautions should be taken to safeguard the company assets and properties.

Day in and day out we hear about a number of scams involving crores of rupees. By taking proper precautionary measures, such loss could have been avoided in every scheme, whether old or new. That is where the ingenuity of a financial manager lies. There is no good in allowing various scams to occur under one's very nose and explaining later how they occurred. Also, it will be worse still if we block every project under the suspicion that there may be a scam. While executing plans, one should devise means to avoid any fraud and implement the projects to the benefit of the organisation and public at large.

We have learnt from all these couplets the essence of financial management. How to get finance for the organisation, how to allocate funds against each item of expenditure by proper budgeting and also the necessity of matching financial progress with physical progress and safeguarding the money from pilferage etc. Managers may make use of the principles enunciated for maximising profits.

Decision Making

DECISION MAKING is an important assignment as well as prerogative of a manager. Every decision taken by a manager affects the performance as well as the image of the organisation. Managers should learn to take correct decisions at the appropriate moment. Thiruvalluvar guides us in taking right decisions.

Prior Thinking

First couplet I would like to discuss here is:

Think first and then venture on an act;
To venture and then think is a fault.

Kural 467

This is a very useful advice for managers. Before devising a plan to carry out any scheme, the manager should think in detail about the pros and cons of all the elements involved and then take a decision. It may result in the loss of money, manpower and image. In this context, we can quote the English proverb, 'Think before you act'.

Any deed without proper efforts and methods
fails despite so many supporters.

Kural 468

When we decide to embark on a project, it is not an end in itself. We should have a definite and detailed plan of execution. Without proper plan, one cannot carry out a job and complete the same successfully. Without a well-conceived plan, the job will not succeed.

Men of wisdom won't embark on anything
and lose their capital to gain something.

Kural 463

The same couplet we have already discussed in financial management. We have come across cases of people being lured by advertisements, quoting high rates of interest and investing in such companies and losing their entire capital.

Taking a Decision

This *Thirukkural* couplet not only applies to financial investments but other cases as well. It applies to men, machinery, goodwill and other assets.

Who dread doing disgraceful errors
won't go in for doubtful ventures.

Kural 464

This is another important aspect in taking a decision. What one is going to do should be made clear in all aspects before taking up any work. It is not possible to pause at every stage and think whether to continue, and if so, how. It may lead to delay. As such, it is necessary that every aspect of the work is made crystal clear before taking up the same for execution.

Do the deeds according to the nature of people.
Or else, even doing good may lead to evil.

Kural 469

This couplet well applies to posting of personnel. We may think we are doing something good to some individual while posting him to a particular place. But it may not suit the individual, based on his domestic circumstances, or the individual may find it difficult to attune himself to that place. As such, instead of doing good to the organisation the placement may lead to conflict and constrain for the concerned beneficiary. In order to avoid such conditions we have to study the habits and character of each individual and act accordingly. This applies not only to an individual but also to the groups and also to the customers.

Let Merit Decide

It's ruinous to do what is not worth doing.
And also not to do what's worth doing.

Kural 466

This is a good lesson for decision-makers. They have to take decision in a reasonable time. Doing a wrong thing at a wrong moment spoils the job. We should not desist from doing things in the required correct manner. Because, if we fail to do right things at the right moment, they will also spoil the job on hand. Therefore, a decision taker should be careful in deciding what to do and what not to do. We have to take care of commission as well as omission.

Deliberate Before Decision

Deliberate and do what the world will approve.
Or else your act the world won't approve.

Kural 470

This is also a point to be reckoned with, before taking a decision to commence a work. What we are going to do should be respected by experts in the world. If it is going to be susceptible to reproach and not acceptable, it is better we refrain from doing such things.

Act only after taking into account
the input, output and result.

Kural 461

This may sound to be an apt advice for taking decisions on financial matters. But actually, this covers the whole gamut of decision taking.

Before taking up a work one should think about what is to be done before taking up that work, what is to be created after that work and what are the direct benefits or spinoff benefits after that work is completed. By taking all these things into consideration he should take a decision whether to take up that project and also when, where and how!

Weighing Implications is Important

When taking up irrigation and hydel projects, forest

wealth may have to be destroyed, hill tribes may have to be rehabilitated and animals have to be displaced. On the other hand, if irrigation potential is created we can grow more and feed more. Electric power is generated on a permanent basis. This helps in establishing more industries, more agricultural pump-sets and with it more ancillary industries may crop up during execution as spin-off benefits. All these things are to be considered and a decision arrived at.

Nothing is impossible to those who understand
the nature and means of the deed.

Kural 472

This is also an important lesson in decision taking. One should take into consideration his/her capacity, what he/ she can do and to what extent? If one decides on this, one should also consider how to go about it and how far. Only after considering all these things should one take a decision. If one takes a decision after due deliberations, nothing can hamper its successful completion. A decision taker should also bear in mind the following couplet.

It is always easy to preach something
but hard to practice the same thing.

Kural 664

Pragmatism

Many people may advise you to do so many things. Many others will advise you on the methodology to be adopted in carrying out the same. But it is always difficult to act as advised. A manager should take this fact into consideration when others advise him. Only when he is satisfied that a particular job or a particular method is practically feasible, should he take up a project.

This *Thirukkural* stresses that pragmatism should prevail while decisions are considered. It is an achievement of a particular job which is more important. Application of mind is required.

Whatever people desire, they get as desired
if only they have firmness of mind.

Kural 666

This couplet stresses that a decision taker should be strong in mind. Only when he is strong in mind he will be able to achieve the objectives. The decision he takes also depends on how strong is his mind, which is a predisposition for taking hard decisions.

After all, a decision is considered as good only when it is implemented in full and the objective is achieved.

A manager who grasps the essence of all these couplets becomes a good decision maker.

Case Studies

To start with, let us see some cases in which skills were utilised to improve human relations.

Case Study 1

In Chennai, one Mr Ramanathan was living in a middle-class residential colony in Adyar. His neighbour, a Mr Sambasivam was a musician. He used to take part in performances held in various Sabhas in Chennai and elsewhere.

Relation between Ramanathan and Sambasivam was just 'smile while you see'. Ramanathan wanted to improve relations with his musician neighbour.

School final exams for Ms Revathy, Ramanathan's daughter were to be held shortly. She was preparing for the exams in full swing. Ramanathan was also doing his best to help her. At that time, Sambasivam was also practising vigorously for his performance. He had been invited by the prestigious Vidwath Sabha to conduct a musical performance on an auspicious day. Sambasivam started practicing intensely ten days before his performance. This disturbed Revathy who was preparing for school final exams. When Ramanathan was actually thinking of improving relations with Sambasivam, here was a chance to spoil the relations.

Ramanathan thought about it positively. When his daughter was preparing for her school final exams, Sambasivam was preparing for his Vidwath Sabha performance. It was quite natural. However, the problem needed to be solved in an amicable manner. Therefore, he wrote a letter to Sambasivam:

Dear Mr Sambasivam, my hearty congratulations to you for having been invited to perform at the Vidwath Sabha. With your knowledge and talents, I know you will come out with flying colours.

In this connection, I take this opportunity to point out that my daughter Revathy is preparing for her school final exams with our assistance and guidance. If you can intimate us of your practising hours, it will be possible for us to suitably reallocate her study schedule. We will be glad to have your reply as soon as possible.

This letter was sent through a messenger. After going through this letter, Sambasivam understood the position and rescheduled his practicing hours so that it may not affect his neighbour. A source of friction was thus converted into a source of friendship by skillful communication.

Weigh and utter your words very well.
That no virtue and wealth can excel.

Kural 644

As Ramanathan understood the meaning of the couplet and used words in his letter carefully, after weighing what exactly he was writing, he was able to find a solution for improving relations rather than spoiling them. The couplet, when applied properly, can help in a number of occasions.

Case Study 2

Let us go to another case of application of the couplets on successful communication. I sent my son to a shop to get a cap for me. He brought a cap which he considered as good. However, I was not satisfied with the cap. I wanted to send it back to the shop through my son, stating that it was not to my satisfaction.

The shop owner was a good friend of mine. When the cap was returned he might think I was criticising his shop and material. A cap is a personal item. In fact, I should have gone in person and got a cap to suit my taste. As such, it was actually my own fault in not getting a cap of my choice.

Therefore, I went to the shop in person and told him that the newly-designed cap given by him was not suitable for my old-fashioned clothes and gave it back to him. I chose a suitable cap out of the stock available with him to suit my taste. My personal visit not only helped me to have a better bargain but also to maintain and improve my relationship with my shop-keeper friend.

Case Study 3

Now let us analyse the case of parents and a child. Balasubramaniam was a professor in a local college at Madurai. His wife Shyamala was working as an assistant in a bank.

Their only child, Sankar was studying in the fourth standard. Both, Balasubramaniam and Shyamala were worried about their child. In their opinion he was very indisciplined. He did not go to school regularly. He never listened to his parents. If the parents wanted him to have his breakfast he would go to the garden to play. When they wanted him to study, he would say he was hungry. Whatever he was asked to do, he would not. This was especially true when his father gave him instructions. Sankar's parents found the situation deteriorating. Somehow they wanted to improve their relations with their child.

One day Balasubramaniam's colleague, Krishnan came to their house. He was a Professor of Psychology in his college. He closely observed what was going on between the parents and the child. Finally, Balasubramaniam complained a lot about his son's disobedient response.

After Sankar went to play in the garden, Krishnan suggested it was up to Bala and his wife to bring about necessary changes in Sankar's behaviour. Balasubramaniam said, 'I have been very strict with him. Even then, I have not been able to change him. What else do you suggest?' Krishnan said: 'It is your strictness that is making him disobedient. The harsh words you use and your tone and punishment put together make him more defiant. Hereafter, you better ask your wife to give him instructions. Harsh words will not be of any use. You better try sweet words. Some acts of kindness and sweet words will work wonders. Try them for a week. The results will be fine. If you don't get the desired results, you better inform me. Let us try to work out a better strategy.' He went away with these words.

For the next two to three days, Balasubramaniam avoided issuing instructions to his son. His wife used kind words in a suggestive tone, instead of commanding tone. Balasubramaniam also tried to talk gently to the child. After a few days, there was a perceptible improvement in Sankar's behaviour. He started following the instructions of his parents. He also showed interest in talking to his parents and spending some time with them. The parents were very happy and conveyed their thanks to Krishnan. Krishnan said: 'I told you what Thiruvalluvar has said two thousand years ago. Those couplets hold good for ever.'

Using bitter words instead of pleasant words
is like preferring unripe fruits to ripe ones.

Kural 100

Case Study 4

Now let us take the case of Ramlal, an assistant engineer of Gujarat State Electricity Board. He is a very duty-conscious, hard-working and efficient engineer. There is no doubt about it. He is also quick to redress the grievances of the consumers of his area. However his relations with his boss, the Superintending Engineer, is not up to the mark. Whenever his Superintending Engineer goes over to his office on inspection, Ramlal is not able to brief him properly regarding his various activities. He is also not able to answer the boss's questions in a satisfying manner. This created a bad opinion in the mind of his Superintending Engineer. How to change his opinion? How to improve Ramlal's relations with his boss? Here his immediate boss, the Executive Engineer, comes to his rescue. He personally knows how sincere Ramlal is. He has also seen how Ramlal has not been able to impress his Superintending Engineer. So the Executive Engineer gives Ramlal some advice.

'What is your problem Ramlal? As soon as you see the Superintending Engineer, you get frightened. That is the root cause of all your problems. You are a hard-working and sincere officer. Then why should you get frightened of your boss? The Superintending Engineer is also a human being like you and me. Therefore, be bold when you see him. Don't get frightened. Immediately on seeing him, put up a brave face and smile, which will disarm anybody.'

The Executive Engineer continued, 'Prepare yourself well for the boss' visit. Regarding your various activities and future plans, be prepared with what you are going to tell him. Avoid any loose words, even casually. Take enough care in this regard. Also, whenever he asks questions, do not get afraid. Answer him clearly to the extent you know. I hope a sincere man like you can win his heart.'

Keeping this piece of advice in his mind, during the next visit of his Superintending Engineer, Ramlal spoke up with some confidence and told the boss all that had happened in his work area. Soon Ramlal found that there was some improvement in the boss' understanding. After two or three visits, Ramlal was able to fully convince his Superintending

Engineer of his sincerity and the various activities carried out by him in the interest of the organisation. Then on, wherever the Superintending Engineer went for inspection, he cited Ramlal as an example for hard and sincere work. He wanted other engineers to emulate Ramlal's example.

Always utter fruitful words.
Never utter futile words.

Kural 200

Gain or loss depends on one's words.
So guard against slip of tongue.

Kural 642

A sound advice in Thiruvalluvar's words, quoted by his immediate boss, gave proper direction to Ramlal and helped him improve his organisational relations.

Case Study 5

Another case we are going to discuss here is the case of a public sector undertaking of the Government of India at Trichy in Tamil Nadu. Some years ago, the organisational relations were at the lowest ebb and the industry was at a loss. The industries ministry wanted to improve the performance of the undertaking. The first step was to improve the interpersonal relations within the organisation. Hence, one Mr Krishnan was posted as Chairman cum Managing Director of that organisation. He is known for his all-round skills.

Immediately on taking over as CMD he held discussions with all the officers and enlisted their cooperation in improving inter departmental relations. He found time to talk with even the junior-most staff to ensure all round cooperation. If anybody had an appointment with him in his chamber, he would go out and invite him into his room, irrespective of his status or stature. Whenever this was not possible, he would stand up and receive the guest.

His attitude and action ensured substantial improvement within the organisation. Even though there were some cynics who viewed his action as gimmick, by and large, people concerned appreciated his efforts and there was cooperation from all departments. Eventually introduction of modern methods in production became feasible and effectively done. Consequently, there was a definite improvement in the performance of the organisation and the undertaking was able to export equipment and execute foreign contracts, improving the foreign exchange reserves of the country.

For all these achievements, Krishnan made the whole teams concerned responsible and gave them awards and appreciation instead of taking credit himself. Such humility earned him name and fame inside and outside the organisation. The performance of the undertaking soared.

Humility is surely a great virtue for one and all.
To the wealthy it is another wealth above all.

Kural 125

The world will always be quick to execute
the words that are sweetly well set.

Kural 648

Humility and sweet words are one's jewels.
All others are not at all jewels.

Kural 95

Fruitful, polite and pleasant words
beget happiness and fortunes.

Kural 97

Krishnan adopted PR techniques which he appeared to have learnt from Thiruvallavar's couplets. They were effective in improving organisational relations and eventually the all round performance of the organisation.

Case study 6

We do know of different kind of environment in some other organisations. Here the bosses humiliate their employees by using offensive language day in and day out. The effect is disastrous. The self-respect of every individual in an organisation should be maintained. Humiliation should be avoided. Humiliation lowers one's morale and undermines his/her self-respect. A person's dislike of the boss often turns into dislike of the organisation. Hence an employee's performance lowers.

Gain or loss depends on one's words.
So guard against slip in words.

Kural 642

If officials heed Thiruvalluvar's advice, given a long time ago, unpleasant incidents can be averted. Also, we have a couplet already, stating,

Kind words with a smiling face
are better than gifts of grace.

Kural 92

We see how the same couplets apply to different cases. Now let us take the case of a debt collector. The job of a debt collector is something which nobody likes. A debt collector is generally hated by people. But the case of Somasundaram from Madurai was quite different. He was liked by everybody, including those from whom he was collecting debts! Various businessmen, industrialists and money lenders gave him the hard task of collecting their non-collectable debts. Somasundaram was very successful.

He never used violent methods. How is it he was successful? Whenever he approached a person to collect a debt, he used courteous and supporting words. He understood that only because of some problems that the person is not able to repay his/her debt. He always asked people about their actual problems, which came in the way of clearing their debts. Listening to them, he sympathised with them and accepted their problems as genuine. He also stressed the importance of clearing the debts as debtors do have their own problems. He discussed with them various method of solving their problems and offered them practical solutions. He also offered to help people who accepted his solution to start repaying their debts. As he helped them in solving their problems, people began to trust him and develop a liking towards him.

This is a case where an intelligent man converts a distasteful job into an interesting and helpful profession.

By fair means seek and secure grace.
All codes proclaim it as assistance.

Kural 242

Painful poverty will never embrace those
who with sweet words cheer others.

Kural 94

Though the help received is millet small
the worthy deem it palm-tree tall.

Kural 104

Somasundaram's success as a debt-collector by improvement in human relations will seem to be the result of application of the above couplets.

Case Study 7

Let us see how the relations between couples can be improved.

Life bereft of love is like a tree sapless
sprouting in utter barrenness.

Kural 78

Couples who love each other are naturally the happiest. One who loves his spouse expects him/her to return the same in equal measure, if not manifold. Love should not be nurtured inside the heart alone. It should be expressed unequivocally so that the others understand the same.

Parimal Gupta and Urmila Gupta found that their relationship had become dull and drab.

Both of them were employed. They had two kids. Their offices, parents and children and social activities were taking their whole time. They did not find time to spend with each other, nor show their love and affection for each other.

In a sudden expression of love, one day Parimal found in his shirt pocket a note, 'I love you' written by his wife. When he returned home, he brought her, her favourite flowers. Thus commenced their renewal of love. They found time to spend with each other inside and outside the home. Once in a week, they went for a picnic or a film or a musical or some other entertainment. Parimal made it a point to drop Urmila to her office and also to bring her back from her office whenever feasible. This way, they found more time to be together. This removed the dullness in their relationship and helped them to improve their marital relations as a mature couple. Their family life naturally became a standing example of what Thiruvalluvar has expressed in his couplet in his inimitable style.

If domestic life has love and virtue
there will be grace and gain true.

Kural 45

Case Study 8

Now let us see how a great leader developed his relationship with the public. Lenin was a mass leader. He was a darling of millions, very like our Jawaharlal Nehru.

Having won the revolution, Lenin was leading the Soviet government. Clara Jedhin describes how Lenin used to listen to those who come to talk to him. 'Lenin was a very good listener. He never lost patience, neither got tired or bored when listening to others. Even for small details he used to lean to the front to hear us properly.' Thiruvalluvar has described the art of listening as:

Listening is the wealth of wealth.
It is the crown of all wealth.

Kural 411

Such listening shows regard towards the speaker and also the interest the listener takes in the subject. Lenin used to give regards to even an ordinary citizen and converse with him freely. Alberrise Williams, who once went to see him, narrates the following incident:

'We had to wait for some time to meet Mr Lenin. But this was something unusual. Lenin generally kept his timings. He was very punctual. Therefore, we thought that he was discussing some subject of national interest with some important minister or officer. Therefore we chose to wait for some more time. However, when the door opened, an ordinary farmer, very ordinarily dressed came out of his room.

'We were surprised to note that he was giving importance even to such ordinary people and listened to them. Such discussions were helpful to him in approaching problems from different angles, so as to arrive at the best solution.

'Lenin directed his officers not to force the farmers to adopt new agricultural methods, but to explain to them and demonstrate their good effects so that they could adopt them in due course. Lenin's advice reminds us of the following Thirukkural couplet:

Who cannot live in harmony with the world
though learned, are fools indeed.

Kural 140

Wisdom is to live in tune with the mood
of the changing world.

Kural 426

As the steps taken by Lenin and the advice given by him to his officials were harmonious for the world, Lenin was accepted as a world leader and was able to develop and maintain best of relations with people at large like our great leader Mahatma Gandhi.

Case Study 9

Language counts not only for a leader but also for salesmen. A reputed company engaged a number of salesmen. One salesman was an expert in languages. He had a very fine vocabulary. His phonetic style was excellent. With his command of language he could keep educated audiences spellbound. Another salesman in the same firm could use only simple, colloquial language.

It was this second salesman who was number one in sales figure. With his limited vocabulary, how was he able to manage so well? His language was simple, direct and courteous. His tone was also pleasing. Instead of making either the product or himself the centre of attention, he made his customers the centre of attention. It was this strategy which won him the first place.

Fruitful, polite and pleasant words
begets happiness and fortunes.

Kural 97

The same principle was applied by the British Milk Marketing Society successfully. Its original slogan in its countrywide advertisement was 'Drink a pint of milk a day'. It was more or less like an order. People did not like to take that command. Later on, the slogan was converted to: 'Drinka pinta milka day'. It blunted the sharp edge of the previous command. The courteous kindly words were fruitful in improving the sales.

Case Study 10

Let us see the success story of Arthur Ashe, the American tennis star of yesteryear. He owes his success as a human being and tennis star to his father Arthur, who developed and maintained the best of relations with his children. Arthur Ashe has said, 'my father's sense of discipline was simple. He knew what was best for his children. And he had only to give an order once. One of his commandments was, there should be no loafing. If he is not working or has gone on some special assignment, man is supposed to be at home.

When the children were in school, Arthur Sr. knew the time taken to get back home and questioned his children if they were late.

He taught his children values of gaining by helping others. He helped the needy, along with his children. He also advised his children not to make enemies because it never worked. He also told them unequivocally, without a good name they would be nothing. It meant they were letting everybody down, their family, friends and history.

Arthur Ashe's mother not only taught the children to read at home but also good manners.

Such being the spirit and initiative taken by the parents, the children achieved success. Arthur Sr. groomed Arthur Ashe as a tennis player under the guidance of Robert Walter Johnson. Apart from developing his basic skills, Johnson helped him develop himself mentally. He taught him not to lose his temper under any circumstances. Being angry at umpires and the opponent player was a waste of energy, Ashe was taught.

As Arthur remained calm and cool, his opponents went to pieces. Arthur Ashe won a number of grand slam titles between 1968 and 1975. Whenever he played, he was known to have cared deeply about all other players.

Arthur Ashe was playing against Nastase for the 1975 Masters Tennis Tournament in Stockholm, Sweden. Nastase was not able to control himself as Ashe was leading. He stalled, cursed and taunted Ashe. When at a point where he could not take it any more, Arthur Ashe said, 'I will leave as

I'm afraid I'll lose my cool'. The Umpire told him, 'You are ahead. If you leave now, you will lose the match by default'. Ashe preferred to lose the match rather than his self-respect. The next day, the tournament committee met. They observed that by disqualifying Arthur Ashe they would be condoning Nastases' bullying tactics. So they decided that it was Nastase who must default the match for his misconduct. It was Ashe's self respect which won him the match which he could have otherwise won by his talents.

All good wishes are obtained instantly
if one's thoughts are ire-free.

Kural 309

Even during his last days, when he was down with AIDS, Ashe helped deprived children, worked to give shelter to Haitian refugees, fought against social injustice and joined the battle against AIDS. What a successful man he was!

Fathers's responsibility to his son lies
in placing him ahead of scholars.

Kural 67

Had not Arthur Senior taken up his duty to make Arthur Ashe a top star in the tennis courts would we have had a Arthur Ashe? He has imbibed good morals in the hearts of his children as Thiruvalluvar has correctly remarked.

If domestic life has love and virtue
there will be grace and gain true.

Kural 45

Case Study 11

Let us go to Taiwan. Here is a case of development of love and social relations to the benefit of members of the society. It was Datuk Seri Cheng Yen, the nun who was the driving force behind the revival of Buddhist T'Zu Chi (compassion relief), Taiwan's biggest charity, who made it all possible. Cheng Yen's selfless devotion awakened Taiwan to the ancient Buddhist teachings of compassion and charity, which had been lost in the mad rush to prosperity. She has been helping the poor to regain dignity and her prescription for the rich is that the rich can heal themselves by helping the poor. A volunteer has said, 'We give her only time, energy and money because she has restored our conscience'.

Let us recreate a scene in the TZ'u-Chi Buddhist General Hospital in Hualien.

Cheng Yen visits the hospital. She asks Lice, an inpatient undergoing physiotherapy treatment for a stroke, 'How are you today?'

'I still can't move my arm', he sobs. Cheng Yen bows and turns to another patient. Lice does not want Cheng Yen to see him like that, hence he asks Cheng Yen to wait. He slowly raises his trembling hands and forces his palms together in a gesture of prayer. His wife shouts: 'He has done it. He has not been able to do this since his stroke.' Lice thanks Cheng Yen. She tells him, 'It is you who did it'. Here is an example of how love and affection work like magic in curing people. Cheng Yen appears to have made everybody realise the meaning of the following Thirukkural couplets:

Love begets the life of love for others
and amity of excellence it yields.

Kural 74

The loveless grab all for themselves.
The loving give even their bones.

Kural 72

Painful poverty will never embrace those
who with sweet words cheer others.

Kural 94

Case Study 12

Now let us take a case of a destroyer of human relations. This bad quality is envy.

Fortune herself will desert the envious
and direct her sister to the envious.

Kural 167

Who know that envy causes misery,
will do no wrong out of envy.

Kural 164

These two Thirukkural couplets depict the woeful effects of envy.

Let us read a story in this regard. Two sick men occupied the same hospital room. One man, whose bed was adjoining the window, was permitted to sit up in his bed for an hour each afternoon to help drain the fluid from his chest. The other man had to spend his time lying on the bed. Both these men used to chat together for hours. They spoke about their families, neighbours and their jobs. Both of them were seriously ill.

Every afternoon, while sitting up in the bed, the one near the window would describe to the room mate all that he could see outside. This one-hour period was a very happy moment for the sick man in the other bed as his limited vision was widened and enlivened by the activities in the outside world. As the sick man heard the window view described, he visualised a park with a lovely lake. Swans and ducks swam in the water. Children also sailed their paper boats with gay abandon. There were flowers of all beautiful colours in the park. Lovers walked hand in hand. Grand old trees graced the landscape. At a distance, a lovely view of the city sky could also be seen.

As this man besides the window described the view the other sick man would close his eyes and imagine the beautiful scenes. One afternoon the man described a parade of school children passing by. The other one enjoyed the imagination. All of a sudden, envy engulfed the second man. 'Why should the other man have the pleasure of an outside view when he himself did not have any such direct pleasure?' Day by day his envy grew. He started disliking his friend. He wanted to move to the window-side bed.

One night the sick man by the window began to cough. He was choking with the fluid in his chest. He could not locate the button to call for help. The other sick man watched this. He did not want to push the button to call the nurse to save the other man. After a few minutes, the choking man lay still.

Next morning when the nurse came, she found the man besides the window dead due to choking. After the body of his friend was removed, the other man wanted to move to the bed near the window. This was easily agreed to by the hospital authorities. The second man was moved to the bed near the window.

After he was made to lie comfortable, he pushed himself to a sitting position to have a look at the outside world and to have the pleasure of seeing for himself. When he turned towards the window, he was shocked. There was only a blank wall. The other man was describing fine scenes only to make his friend happy. But in return, the friend had let him die, out of sheer envy. As his conscious pricked him, this second man felt miserable and soon died. Envy destroyed both.

Case Study 13

Now let us understand another Kural to note how patience enhances the name and fame of a saint and gets him highest regard in society.

Self-control will place one among gods,
lack of it sinks one into a life of evils.

Kural 121

Self-control guided by wisdom
fetches everlasting fame.

Kural 123

To bear with others' evils is a good trait.
Better it is to forget it.

Kural 152

Conquer men who are arrogant
simply by your tolerance.

Kural 158

The relevance of all these couplets is explained in the following story.

There was a great saint in Maharashtra. He was the personification of patience and peace. He never lost his temper. There were some big people in the town who were jealous of his reputation. Therefore they wanted to prove him otherwise. They hired a man with promise of high rewards to make the saint lose his temper.

Every day the saint used to go to a holy river for a dip and return to his kudil (hut) for pooja. One day, when he was returning to his kudil after his dip, the hired man spat at him. Without any anger, the saint went back to bathe again and returned. The same incident continued for a number of times. The saint never lost patience. It was eventually the man who spat on him, who lost his patience. He felt guilty. He fell at the feet of the saint. He told him the whole truth and asked for his forgiveness.

The saint told him, 'Today you have given me an opportunity to have a holy dip in the river a number of times. You have done something good for me. Had you told me initially that for making me angry you'd get a reward, I would have obliged you'.

There is no doubt why such a man is held in high esteem in society and hailed as a saint. In society, such a saint inspires followers and through them inspires the whole country.

Case Study 14

Let us go to another story which tells us that arrogance leads one to a fall. It is only humility which can protect one.

Long and vain speech trumpets
one's utter worthlessness.

Kural 193

Who utters vain words displeasing all
is despised by one and all.

Kural 191

The following example clearly shows the relevance of above couplets of Thiruvalluvar, the poet-saint of ancient Tamil Nadu.

There was a learned man in Varanasi. He had learnt all the sastras. Even though he was a learned man, people were reluctant to approach him for learning in any sphere. It was because he ridiculed their little knowledge before he started teaching them. They took his words as insult and went to different teachers.

Still this learned man could not overcome his arrogance. He also insulted anybody who came to have a discussion with him on any subject.

One day, he had to go to the other side of the Ganges. He hired a boat for this purpose. He was the lone passenger on the boat. After sometime, the learned man asked the boat man whether he had any kind of formal education. The boat man said, 'My father was a poor man and could not afford to send me to school. I can't read or write. I am an ordinary boatman'. The learned man said, 'one third of your life is a waste. Have you at least heard our Itikathas Ramayana and Mahabharata?' The boatman said, 'No sir. I have not heard the stories even though I know their names'.

The learned man said, 'What a sinful soul you are! Two third of your life is a waste'.

Sometime later, when they reached the middle of the river there was a storm. It was about to upset the boat.

The boatman asked the learned man, 'O Master, can you swim? The boat is going to turn upside down. We have to jump aboard, swim and escape'. 'No, No. I do not know swimming', said the learned man.

The boatman said, 'O master, your whole life is going to be a waste', and he jumped into the river, swam and escaped. The saying goes, 'Pride goes before a fall'.

Case Study 15

We have heard the story of Jean Val Jean. The pastor with a high degree of compassion helped a man, even though he stole silver articles from his house. There is a similar story for which Thirukkural couplets are relevant.

Love helps only virtue, say the unwise.
It also guards us from all evils.

Kural 76

Men of mercy who guard all beings
are free from fear of evils.

Kural 244

By fair means seek and secure grace.
All codes proclaim it as assistance.

Kural 242

Giving to the poor alone is real charity.
All else aim at recompense only.

Kural 221

A saint was chanting holy hymns in his cottage one evening. Then a thief entered his cottage. He demanded from the saint all his money. The saint calmly told him, 'I'm chanting hymns to God. Do not disturb me. The money is inside the box there. Go and take whatever you want'. Then he started chanting hymns once again. Then he remembered something and told the thief, 'Do not take all the money, we have to pay some taxes tomorrow. So please leave two hundred rupees'.

The thief took most of the money and started leaving.

'Thank a person when you receive a gift', the saint told him. The thief thanked him and left the cottage.

After a few days the thief was caught by the police. He confessed about his theft in the saint's house along with the other thefts and burglaries committed by him. The saint was questioned by the police. He told them, 'As far as I am concerned, this man is not a thief. I gave him the money. He also thanked me for it'.

The thief, after serving his imprisonment, came to the saint along with his friends. He told the saint that he was transformed by his words and along with his friends he had come to the saint to become his disciples.

The saint's behaviour and development of good relations even with a thief made them transform themselves into honourable members of the society.

Case Study 16

Now let us analyse an incident which happened in Mysore with the aid of the following *Thirukkural* couplets.

Knowing their worth, Fortune stays with the wise
who value virtue and covet not riches.

Kural 179

Who seek eternal happiness
for petty joys, do no evil acts.

Kural 173

Inordinate passion for thieving
Results in endless suffering.

Kural 284

The late Maharaja of the princely state of Mysore was a lover of flower shows. Once he visited a flower garden. He enjoyed the sight of all the flowers and was specially attracted by lovely roses. He spent some time standing before them and admired them for their beauty. After going around the garden, he returned to his car to depart. Then the superintendent of the garden brought a bunch of roses and presented them to the Maharaja of Mysore. He thought that the Maharaja would appreciate him for the gesture. But he was disappointed.

The Maharaja said, 'You have committed a wrong act. In order to curry favours with me, you have deprived many visitors of the pleasure of seeing the roses and enjoying the beautiful sight. You better avoid such selfish acts, at least in the future'.

Is it not correct that wrong and greed will bring only grief and pain as suggested in the *Thirukkural?* The Maharaja, who cared about people at large, was held in high esteem by the society. All these cases clearly show us how to develop, improve and maintain proper human relations and also that success and respect are the benefits of such improved relations.

Case Study 17

For a business concern, marketing strategy involves analysis of various factors, based upon which the company decides what the people would like to have tomorrow.

For instance, a pressure cooker manufacturer (Rampur & Co) was manufacturing good and sturdy pressure cookers in one particular design. They were compact and safe, and hence a very useful pressure cooker. They were on top.

But people are not necessarily satisfied with that alone. Their conception of pressure cookers was different to what Rampur & Co had in mind. They wanted greater comfort, lightweight and different colours. Premier & Co made a market study and knew what the people wanted. Based on their study, they manufactured different varieties of pressure cookers and sent to the market.

Their hopes were not belied. Their makes made a good turnover in all the markets. They steadily rose to the first position, replacing Rampur & Co.

The customer's point of view is different from that of the producer. A cosmetic maker once said, 'We don't sell cosmetic. We sell Hope, ie. hope of being the most beautiful girl. The product is not simply a product'.

We may think a car is meant for transport. But for an industrialist, it is not simply a mode of transport. It exhibits his wealth and status.The more he rises in the ladder of success, the better model he chooses. Therefore, it is necessary for a car producer to know what the customer wants, even though he is already a manufacturer of a quality product.

However well-versed in performing a deed,
one should tread the way of the world.

Kural 637

This Thirukkural couplet wants you to act after knowing the world's outlook ie. market study in this case.

Case Study 18

For any project, work should be properly planned.Otherwise, workers may be idling without raw materials or tools. Finished products may be idling without any sale orders. All these things may result in a huge loss. Some management experts often cite the example of the famous pottery firm of Wedgwood for good planning. Josia Wedgwood won international fame for his British pottery firm, which has today become a leading pottery producer in the world. He started his industry during the eighteenth century, with a capital of just a few pounds. During that period, management science was neither taught nor propagated. He learnt management by intuition and practised it.

He organised the workshops of his craftsmen into well-knit and compact production units. The employees were offered job security. He mastered the art of blending art with industry. Many well-known artists were engaged by him to give his pottery a good and grand look. He took abnormal interest in sales promotion. He also appreciated art. Therefore, it is not surprising to note he made a big fortune during his lifetime.

Whatever people desire, they get as desired
if only they have firmness of mind.

Kural 666

Nothing is ever impossible for those who act
after wise counsel and careful thought.

Kural 462

These Thirukkural couplets explain how Wedgwood was able to achieve such a phenomenal success.

Case Study 19

Modern management often mentions the term 'workaholic'. These people are totally absorbed in work. They work very hard. They always work without any rest. They also want all their subordinates to work like them. Is it correct for a manager to be a workaholic?

Can workaholics succeed? Let us look into some typical cases.

I have my own experiences in this matter. When I went to replace an officer in the office of the Superintending Engineer, the officer told me he had to deal with a lot of papers and work long hours to clear all of them.

His main duty was to scrutinise the estimates received from the field, to get them sanctioned by the Superintending Engineer and communicate the sanctions to the field. He had three Junior Technical Officers under his control. They used to scrutinise the estimates and put them up to him. After he checked, they were put up to the SE for sanction. On receipt of approval by the SE, he used to sign all communications of sanction to the field. That work took a big portion of his time. He was not able to concentrate on checking the estimates or deal with other important connected papers.

Hence on joining, I decided that it was enough that the communication of sanction to the field was signed by the Junior Officers. It was not an additional work as the above communications were checked by them before being forwarded for my signature. Once this process was set in motion, I found ample time to check up the estimates properly and deal with all the important papers with the attention they deserved. Ultimately, we were able to work efficiently as well as effectively. In a number of cases

workaholism spoils performance, as it affects efficiency.

I, while holding different office posts, had to permit a number of field officers to meet me during office hours, besides a number of consumers. This was unavoidable in the system. As such, I looked at only routine papers during working hours. I dealt with important papers only before office hours, by being in the office a bit early.

One has to take adequate rest when one feels tired. This is necessary to restore energy and enthusiasm. An energetic and enthusiastic man working for six hours can easily be more effective than a dull and drab man working for twelve hours or more. To avoid being a workaholic, one should take to some hobbies. Overwork is not the solution. Diligent work is the only way to be effective.

Delay only the deeds that merit delay.
Delay not deeds that merit no delay.

Kural 672

It's ruinous to do what is not worth doing
and also not to do what's worth doing.

Kural 466

Tho' a cart carries light peacock feathers,
its axle breaks if the load exceeds.

Kural 475

All these couplets indicate why overwork should be avoided. Systematic work is more effective in achieving peak performance.

Case Study 20

Punishment as an instrument, to make people work properly, hardly ever works. Instead, positive reinforcement works well. There were complaints throughout the State of Tamil Nadu that the State Transport Corporation buses did not care about the public. They did not stop even at scheduled stops. Passengers were not cared for.

The transport minister, instead of introducing punishment, thought appropriate to introduce a system of positive reinforcement. The proposal was to give incentive to the driver and conductor, depending on the number of passengers who travelled on the bus. This automatically worked in respect of most of the corporation crew. There were no complaints of not stopping of buses at scheduled stops.

The other reason for not stopping of buses, besides the indifference of the crew, was the short time allotted for the journey. By proper maintenance and repair of the buses, this was managed. The same method worked in respect of the power sector also. Most of the generating stations were in a state of mess. There were frequent shutdowns, both forced and planned. Consequently, the Plant Load Factor (PLF) was very poor. There were frequent load sheddings, leading to public complaints.

Besides analysing other factors, a scheme of incentives was introduced. Minimum PLF was fixed and certain amount of incentive was introduced beyond minimum PLF. This was made applicable to all the employees of the thermal stations. Consequently, the Plant Load Factor went on improving.

It never dropped below the minimum level in almost all the stations. These are two solid examples which show how positive reinforcement works.

Bounty, mercy, justice and love for the subjects
who has all these is a light among monarchs.

Kural 390

This couplet clearly indicates how the government (ruler) can have its way through successful management techniques like positive reinforcement (bounty), care and grace.

Case Study 21

Present-day business involves a number of complexities. All aspects of business have to be taken into consideration before planning any new proposal.

The Jain brothers wanted to venture into new business in Tamil Nadu where they found labour cheap. Parimal Jain wanted to take over some of the sick textile mills and run them efficiently. He put his men on the job and took over six textile mills in various places in Tamil Nadu. He soon found that all the machinery were old and beyond repair. In order to run the mill profitably, almost all the machinery had to be replaced and mills as a whole to be modernised. It needed a lot of capital. If the mills were modernised most of the labour had to be retrenched and there was stiff opposition from the trade unions. Moreover, the government labour law as well as the labour department was against such wholesale retrenchment. Wherever the labour was agreeable huge sums of money had to be paid as retrenchment compensation.

Seeing this, Jain found that a takeover would not be profitable. He wanted to turn back on the proposal but that was also not possible, as he had entered into an agreement with the original owners of the textile mills. This makes it clear that it is necessary to go into the viability of proposals in toto, before actually signing on documents.

Think first and then venture on an act.
To venture and then think is a fault.

Kural 467

Men of wisdom won't embark on anything
and lose their capital to gain something.

Kural 463

These two couplets indicate clearly how daredevil ventures, without proper analysis and thinking, can be avoided.

Case Study 22

This is a story often quoted by management experts. A famous manufacturer of typewriters found that his business was sinking. As people were getting used to computers, the need for typewriters was also diminishing.

He thought he could enter the computer market. But there were several established organisations against whom it would be suicidal to compete. Another way out was to enter the markets of developing countries. Here also, the rules and regulations of the governments of various developing countries were very rigorous. Also, corruption was rampant at the political and bureaucratic level. Therefore, he had to drop that idea too. Finally, he had an idea. He approached a computer manufacturer and offered to supply him typing ancillaries for the computers. A satisfactory arrangement was worked out and he switched over his business to manufacture typing ancillary for computers. Since then, despite his limited resources, his business has bloomed.

Nothing is impossible to those who understand
the nature and means of the deed.

Kural 472

Is there any task not possible for those
who choose right time and means?

Kural 483

These Thirukkural couplets illustrate how the typewriter manufacturer pulled his business out of the woods and made it profitable because he had the necessary knowledge.

Case Study 23

The wise discern what is in store,
but fools luck in that lore.

Kural 427

Do the deeds according to the nature of people.
Or else even doing good may lead to evil.

Kural 469

These couplets expect some sort of anticipation and imagination on the part of the managers.

In a workshop, a number of tools were found missing from the tool room. As the tools required could not be supplied, the job was hampered. Moreover, loss of tools required their replacement, incurring more expenditure. In order to avoid pilferage, the manager devised a system by which the workers were expected to sign two to three forms and registers to get the tools and also for returning the tools. Most of the workers, being uneducated, did not know how to fill in the forms. This resulted in a lot of confusion. Moreover, the workers could not do the job in the end and productivity of the workshop declined.

Some of them refused to sign the forms. They were not given any tools. Neither were they given any job. Consequently, the work suffered. However, they represented to the government labour officer and the company had to pay them wages.

All these undesirable things could have been avoided if the manager had some sense of anticipation and proper knowledge about the workers. He should have introduced procedures suitable to them.

On the other hand, in a similar situation in a different workshop, entry into the workshop was restricted. The tool room was properly protected. It could be approached only through a narrow corridor. A new tool was issued only after the old broken tool was returned. Such a system avoided pilferage. The workers did not sign any forms which they could not read, and hence they did not have anything to object to. The scheme was successful.

This clearly indicates that a manager has to device processes according to the people he manages, as suggested in *Thirukkural*. Also, a wise manager has to foresee the future.

Case Study 24

Get not discouraged saying 'It's hard'.
Efforts will bring due regard.

Kural 611

Waver not on acts resolved but act firmly,
fearlessly and wakefully.

Kural 668

'To ensure success, it is necessary to pursue your goal with consistent efforts. What I quote above tallies with my own experience.' This is narrated by Tom Morris, an English writer as his own experience.

When we analyse the cause of professional failure, we can easily discover that a major cause is behaviour, thought and action inconsistent with personal goals. We see a salesman who wants to become a Sales Manager, being rude to the consumers and failing to achieve his targets. An unemployed man, who wants a job, spends most of his time on entertainment.

Some time back, I wanted to become a writer. I read a lot of literature on this subject and listened to lectures on writing. I also held discussions with a number of senior authors in this field. What I failed to do was to write.

Then I realised that my failure to take the big step was inconsistent with my goal. I started writing consistently and became successful. The single great difference between success and failure is not generally brilliance but persistence. Many brilliant people who are afraid of failure give up after a few falls. But those who persist and get up one more time to try again, succeed. Thiruvalluvar has aptly said, 'one who tries hard, gets the reward'.

Case Study 25

Gain or loss depends on one's words.
So guard against slip of tongue.

Kural 642

When the spoken word is command, one has to be very careful. One should select the proper terms to give the command slogan, because a communication failure while giving a command will be disastrous. To impress the above point, the following incident is reported by world war veterans.

During the last world war, in a scene of combat called Battle-Axe, the following incident took place. One Mr Beresford was the new commander. He was new to tank warfare, and hence, he was not familiar with the jargons. He ordered the tanks to 'rally forward'. That meant they should take position in front of the infantry and guns. The generally used and understood order was 'forward rally', meaning that the tanks should position themselves behind the infantry in order to support the infantry. At the same time, they will also be protected if under attack. Due to wrong command in this battle, out of 104 tanks, 91 tanks were lost by the British Army. The fault of the commander fell on the shoulders of his chief. Lord Wavell, the commander-in-chief, was dismissed by the Prime Minister of England, Winston Churchill. Now, we can understand that one has to be very careful in issuing commands with so much of force behind them. We have to select proper terms to avoid communication failure.

Case Study 26

When rare and ripe opportunity arrives,
venture at once into rare deeds.

Kural 489

This is a good lesson in exploitation of opportunity. They should be found fast and exploited then and there, without loss of time.

Let us try to understand things again through an incident in World War ll. The German Commander, Rommel, operating in Africa, was an expert in exploiting opportunity. He was first defeated in battle and nursing his wounds when an opportunity came. He was informed by one of his reliable officers who carried out reconnaissance on British advance forces that they were in a state of disarray and confusion. Rommel had just received fifty-five tanks from Germany. He launched the attack immediately. His offensive proved to be a great success. It resulted in the fall of the historic fort, Tobruk, in the port city of Libya.

This is in tune with *Thirukkural*, asking one to do rare things daringly at the proper time.

Case Study 27

What is the use of countless millions earned
if it is not shared and enjoyed?

Kural 1005

The following example is cited by many a writer and speaker. David Harris is very famous in the world of software. He developed a sophisticated E-mail programme called Pegasus. The above programme is used by more than five million people on Internet. When most of the software giants were charging multi-million dollar fees, Harris was giving this product free. Let us consider the reasons given by him.

'I believe communication is a basic human right, as basic as freedom of speech. The mail is our expression of freedom of speech. It seems immoral to me that people should have to pay for this right. I get immense satisfaction when I receive a message from an under-school or charity or a poor country, saying that I have given something that they could not otherwise afford. That kind of fulfillment cannot be described. It can only be experienced.'

The art of giving lends perfection to one's life. If it is there in a person, he can really be happy. It also earns glory and fame.

The only benefit in life is glory
that comes of charity.

Kural 231

Case Study 28

Here is a case which has been mentioned by a number of management experts.

Donald Peterson, when he was Chairman of the Ford Motor Company did something remarkable to outsmart the larger General Motors. 'Focus on products, profit will follow' was his principle. One day, when he walked through his design office, he checked with his designers, whether the model on which they were working was up to their satisfaction or not. They replied negatively. Peterson suggested that they better do the designs which excited them. All of us know the result. Out came one of the most wonderful US automobiles of the 1980s, the Ford Taurus.

Peterson pointed out that working for profits alone was like playing tennis with the eye on the scoreboard. If the scoreboard has to click, you have to look at the ball. That is why he gave the designers freedom to design the cars which delighted them. That policy brought success to the company. The design that delighted the designers brought fame and wealth to the firm.

After examining one's fitness for the deed,
employ him for that deed.

Kural 518

Wealth will ask and find its way to him
who has unshaken enthusiasm.

Kural 594

The above couplets explain the success of Peterson and his designers.

Case Study 29

Men overcome even relentless destiny
with their ceaseless industry.

Kural 620

A young man was a door-to-door salesman, selling vacuum cleaners, at the early age of seventeen. He had some miserable experiences.

He was called by a retired department store manager. When he was demonstrating a low-power nozzle for cleaning rings, he stepped behind and tripped over the machine and fell on his back to the ground. He rose again and explained how the powerful suction of the machine could pick up three steel balls weighing half a kilo each. While doing so, a ball dropped on the customer's toe. The customer was sympathetic. He bought one machine. He also advised, 'continue your job, you'll do fine'.

The young man, without losing spirits, visited as many houses as possible. He relied on statistical probability. The more houses he visited, the more demonstrations he was able to do. The more demonstrations he did, the more vacuum cleaners he was able to sell. His untiring efforts paid off. Later, he was promoted into management cadre. Then in 1986, he became the head of his company.

He is none other than Dennis Johnson, Chairman and Chief Executive of Electrol.

Perseverance leads to prosperity.
Effortlessness results in poverty.

Kural 616

This is a solid example of how one who was industrious, prospered due to his efforts.

Case Study 30

Even though misfortune may rise like a flood,
a wise man overcomes it by thoughts bold.

Kural 622

Many of us might have come across this story of a physically handicapped Indian student. Though on crutches, Gopal was of friendly disposition. He won a number of academic honours and earned the respect of his classmates and teachers. One day, one of his classmates asked him the reason for his deformity. Gopal replied that it was due to 'Infantile Paralysis'. The boy then asked Gopal, 'How do you face the world with such a serious handicap and succeed?'

Gopal replied with a smile, 'The disease has affected only my body and not my heart'.

Gopal's example shows us what the *Thirukkural* has told us: that with a strong heart, one can easily face even deluging sorrows.

Case Study 31

Is there any task not possible for those
who choose right time and means?

Kural 483

One day, suddenly, a cyclone hit without warning the area of one of the Junior Engineers (Maintenance). A number of power distribution lines were damaged and poles were uprooted. Even though it was within the jurisdiction of the Junior Engineer (Maintenance), I sensed that due to his limitations, the work for restoration of power supply would be entrusted to me. Therefore, I immediately started getting my organisation ready to face the job. It would take a long time to manufacture reinforced concrete poles that need curing for three weeks. Moreover, such heavy poles could not be transported in that terrain, especially immediately after it was hit by cyclone and floods. Hence, I arranged for rolled steel joists and their reinforcement to suit the terrain. After a week, when the cyclone and floods subsided and as and when the terrain was ready for operation, I was entrusted with the job of restoration of power supply to that remote area. As I was ready with men and materials, we rushed to the site and completed our works and restored supply in a record time. Incidentally, this earned the appreciation of our Chief Engineer not only for me, but also for my subordinate staff as well as superior officers.

Means, time, mode and rare deeds,
a minister is efficient in these.

Kural 631

Thiruvalluvar says that choosing proper means, time and mode results in successful completion of a rare venture. Such type of action brings satisfaction to all those who are involved in the act and the public at large, who are the beneficiaries, besides encouraging others to take similar action in future.

Case Study 32

Bad luck is not at all a fault of anyone,
but lack of lore and effort brings stain.

Kural 618

This couplet teaches us that we should neither be afraid nor ashamed of failures. In fact, we should learn from our failures and try again and again till we succeed.

This is an oft-quoted incident. A gentleman was interested in skating. He used to watch others skating. He was almost an expert in skating from what he knew. But he did not try skating when he was young because he thought that he could trip and fail and it would be ludicrous and others would laugh at him. The fear of failure prevented him from trying. However, when he reached middle age, he took the decision. If he didn't do it then he would never do it. He thought, 'What if I fail? What if I look ridiculous? Why should I care about it? After all, I am satisfying my long felt desire'. After a few failures, he became a fairly successful skater.

Everybody cannot compete with more talented people and come out on the top without proper training.

But anyone can attain self-satisfaction, if he does an act of his choice and fulfill long-felt desire. He may even come up tops in the long run. Without mistake, there is no discovery. There is nothing wrong in being less than perfect when you attempt something new. George Bernard Shaw has remarked, 'A man learns skating by making a fool of himself. In every field, he makes progress only by making a fool of himself'.

One of my friends failed in one subject in his final year engineering exams. He later on passed the same subject with high marks. He attended an interview for a research fellowship. There were Honours and first class students among those who attended the interview. However, the interview committee chose my friend as he fared well. The chairman of the interview committee remarked, 'did your best in the next attempt and came out with flying colours. We need such courageous people'. Instead of blaming him for his failure in the first attempt, the committee was able to appreciate his performance in the subsequent attempt. As stated in *Thirukkural*, these people are never discouraged by failure. They take the next step and succeed.

Case Study 33

Even great scholars free from vice
are seldom free from ignorance.

Kural 503

It has nowadays become a fashion to seek experts' opinion for even simple things. In most of the organisations, communication of information from bottom to top is done through periodical returns.

In one organisation, the volume of such returns was so big that the officers were not able to attend to their work effectively. When the above matter was reviewed by an in-house committee for remedial action, it was found that the above returns were formulated as per the advice of an expert committee which was specially appointed for that purpose. In fact, the committee had not taken into consideration the time needed for the actual work to be carried out by the officers. They had concentrated only on the Management Information System, ignoring the main objective of the organisations. Let us go to one more expert opinion.

A few years ago, the stock market in India showed a downward trend. After some time, I saw a big one-page analysis on investments in a reputed newspaper. The writer quoted a number of things and concluded that stock markets were quite likely to bounce back and investment in mutual funds were the wisest at that time. As the analyst was an expert, I invested rupees one lakh in different mutual funds. Unfortunately, the shares invested then never picked up. The value of Rs 1000 shares had slumped to Rs 370. This clearly shows that even experts can be ignorant or callous. That does not mean that we should always ignore expert opinion. On the other hand, we should not take their opinion at face value. We should also verify it through our intuition and other sources, and then only take a decision.

Case Study 34

They require no ally but fearless might
if a right field they choose to fight.

Kural 497

There was a time when industries were growing fast in Tamil Nadu. Ramanathan Chettiar, a leading industrialist of Tamil Nadu, thought of constructing a factory for the manufacture of gloves. He chose a centre of activity, taking into consideration the availability of raw materials, power, cheap labour and nearness to market from transportation point of view. From that angle, the village he chose was an ideal place. But the industry had to employ skilled workmen and qualified technical and managerial personnel. Most of them quit some time after joining. Qualified people were also not willing to join.

The reason is that these qualified people were looking for good climate, schools, health care and decent locality. As these facilities were not available, the industry had to run with fifty per cent of the staff. In order to motivate them to continue, the management had to build these facilities at a huge cost. Under the circumstances, the industry was not commercially viable.

However, his brother-in-law, Sevugan realised that qualified people naturally prefer quality of life. As such, he established his factory very near Coimbatore city, where all the facilities were available. Hence, all his employees stuck to their jobs. He did not have to spend a lot of money on building facilities. As industries can be located anywhere in a suitable place nowadays, his industry was commercially viable. As he rightly chose the proper place, as suggested in the *Thirukkural*, he was able to succeed.

Case Study 35

The world will always be quick to execute
the words that are sweetly well set.

Kural 648

Select and speak only such words
not excelled by other words.

Kural 645

Sir Winston Churchill is an outstanding example of an astute orator. During World War II, he mesmerised the

British people and kept their morale high. They were highly motivated by his inspiring words and were prepared to sacrifice their all for the country. His greatest speech 'Blood, Sweat and Tears' is recalled even today. He rose to great heights mainly because he learnt, practiced and mastered the skills of oratory. He prepared his speech to suit the audience. He used to rehearse his speeches in the bathroom. Once his valet thought that Churchill was calling him from his bathroom. Expecting some urgency, the valet entered his bathroom and asked whether he needed any help. 'No' said Churchill, 'I wasn't talking to you. I was addressing the House of Commons'.

If you want to make a winning speech, you have to practice to choose the proper words and proper style.

Those with pure mind and studied eloquence
should use words that suit the audience.

Kural 711

Sir Winston Churchill employed this technique. He adapted styles and words suitable to the audience and occasions while speaking in the House of Commons or at a public forum.

Case Study 36

Whatsoever is heard, from whomsoever
to discern the truth is wisdom clear.

Kural 423

What I am going to narrate here is an oft-repeated incident. A bus went underneath a bridge. At one point, it got sandwiched between the bridge and the ground where the height was at the lowest. The driver was thinking seriously about some plans to get the bus out. As usual, a crowd assembled there. A number of people gave their suggestions. Most of them contained major modifications to the bridge, ground or the bus.

A small boy came upt with an idea. He suggested that some air be let out of the tyres and the bus be moved in reverse gear. Finally, it was that suggestion which worked.

Most of us would have heard about brainstorming sessions in a number of organisations. If we get more number of ideas, the possibility of getting a good idea is more. This is what the *Thirukkural* had suggested two thousand years ago and the suggestion remains in this world forever.

End Note

Now the readers have gone through all the chapters and have discovered what Thiruvalluvar wrote two thousand years ago is still relevant for the managers of the day.

The management techniques prescribed by Thiruvalluvar is helpful not only in professional but also in personal life. When we want to manage a given situation, *Thirukkural* comes to our aid.

This is because management in any day, whether it is yesterday, today or tomorrow is based on common sense. Without common sense, nobody can survive.

This common sense *Thirukkural* has in abundance. That is why the teachings in *Thirukkural* are still relevant.

Apart from common sense, *Thirukkural* deals at length with human values. Even though these human values may have undergone a change, the basic human values are still intact. Any individual or society which holds human values high on the agenda is bound to succeed in the long run. It is on this basic assumption that *Thirukkural* gives us successful management techniques.

Similarly, we can see management concepts, based on common sense and human value, enshrined in all the moral books in Tamil.

As recommended by Thiruvalluvar, a manager should have all the good qualities to succeed. While maintaining high principles of integrity, he should be pragmatic in order to mould humane and civilised organisations. A manager should be able to motivate all around him. Motivation brings success because it facilitates teamwork. It makes every member realise the objectives of the organisation and do his duty before claiming his portion of the cake.

We can achieve very good results in our professional as well as personal lives, if we apply the management techniques recommended in *Thirukkural*. A reading of this book will bring success to the readers in their efforts to manage their professional as well as personal lives.